Søren Kierkegaard

a biographical introduction

Ronald Grimsley

Studio Vista London

Other books by Ronald Grimsley

Existentialist Thought Cardiff 1955
Jean-Jacques Rousseau: a study in self-awareness Cardiff 1961
Jean d'Alembert (1717–83) Oxford 1963
Søren Kierkegaard and French Literature Cardiff 1966
Rousseau and the Religious Quest Oxford 1968
etc., etc.

The photograph used in the front cover design is reproduced by courtesy of the Radio Times Hulton Picture Library, London.

© Ronald Grimsley 1973

Published in Great Britain by Studio Vista
Blue Star House, Highgate Hill, London N19

Set in Times 327 9 point solid
Printed by Richard Clay, Chaucer Press, Bungay, Suffolk

ISBN 0 289 70180 5 (paperback)
ISBN 0 289 70181 3 (hardback)

Kierkegaard: a biographical introduction

Leaders of Modern Thought

Series Editor: Christine Bernard

This Series is primarily designed for senior school and university students who are studying sociology, history, economics, politics and medicine, yet whose work at some time crosses the disciplines of psychology, literature and philosophy.

The authors writing for this Series, all specialists in their own field, approach the subject of their study from a biographical point of view; they are as concerned with fact as with theory. They introduce the subject's growth, development and discoveries as they relate to his background, family, friends and teachers, within the context of his life, rather than as abstractions of fully-matured theories.

The first three published titles in the Series were NIETZSCHE by Janko Lavrin, SARTRE by Philip Thody and FREUD by Penelope Balogh. Two new studies appear alongside Ronald Grimsley's KIERKEGAARD: ALDOUS HUXLEY by Philip Thody and HO CHI MINH by Charles Fenn.

Contents

Acknowledgements:

Thanks are due to the Princeton University Press for permission to use English translations of Kierkegaard's works, full details of which are given in the bibliography at the end of this volume, and to Dr Alexander Drew for permission to use his translation of *The Journals*.

1 Early Influences

At first sight Kierkegaard is an almost classical example of a writer whose psychological development was determined from his earliest years by the overwhelming influence of one of his parents. When he was born in Copenhagen on 5 May 1813, his parents were already middle-aged, his mother being forty-five and his father, Michael Pedersen Kierkegaard, already fifty-six. Søren Aabye was their seventh and last child. In later life Kierkegaard rarely mentions his mother, Ane Sørensdatter Lund, who had been a servant in the Kierkegaard house and had married the master within a year of his first wife's death; she seems to have been a cheerful, equable and simple woman, without much culture and apparently never able to understand her children's intellectual interests. It was, however, the father who was to dominate his youngest child's whole existence. Michael Pedersen Kierkegaard was a strange, brooding, domineering man, torn between powerful passion (it would seem that he had been intimate with his second wife before their marriage, for a child was born five months after the wedding) and an equally strong religious need. After spending a poverty-stricken childhood in Jutland, he was never able to forget the terrible occasion when, as a child tending sheep on the heath, he had once cursed God during one of his lonely and unhappy vigils. Sent to Copenhagen to live with an uncle who ran a prosperous business, he eventually became involved in the wool trade (he was described as a 'hosier') and was so successful that he retired at the early age of forty. Part of his fortune, it is true, had been due to good luck: he had invested his money in government bonds at a time when all other bonds suffered serious depreciation during a national monetary crisis. He then turned to intellectual and religious pursuits (he was particularly fond of the German philosopher Wolff), but his material prosperity, which astonished him, caused him to take an increasingly pessimistic view of life, and he came to believe that his family had been marked down by God for an untimely end: he was convinced that his children would eventually disappear without trace. Indeed, the early death of several of them confirmed his fear that none would live to be more than thirty-three (Christ's age). (Søren himself believed that he would die young, and was genuinely surprised when he celebrated his thirty-fourth birthday). Michael Kierkegaard followed for a time the Moravian Brothers, but then came under the influence of a famous priest, Mynster, whom he made his spiritual guide and mentor. Michael Kierkegaard's Christianity placed its main emphasis upon Christ's suffering rather than his compassion. This 'melancholy old man', as his son described him, was responsible for the religious education of a boy who was 'humanly speaking, insanely brought up' on a strict and rigid Christian outlook. The figure of Christ on the Cross was to make an indelible impression on the child's mind, and may have helped to develop feelings of guilt and melancholy at an early age: in any case, young Søren was subjected to a very strong moral influence during his first years. Moreover, the father's influence also helped to develop a persistent habit of introspection and self-analysis: 'he early became accustomed to occupy himself with himself and his own thoughts'.[1] Of his childhood he was later to say that his life began 'without immediacy, with a terrible melancholy',[2] which prevented him from knowing the joyful, spontaneous activity of normal children. Even so, he always had a very great respect and affection for his father, to whom he was later to dedicate his *Edifying Discourses*, and to whom he was indebted for his understanding of divine, as well as human, love.

As a child, Søren was to be impressed not only by his father's religious principles but also by his 'glowing imagination'. When he wanted to go for a walk, his father would take him by the hand and 'walk back and forth in the room', vividly describing, as he did so, the various sights and sounds of the outside world. 'After half an hour of such a walk with his father he was as much overwhelmed and fatigued as if he had been a whole day out of doors'.

The Copenhagen of Kierkegaard's day bore little resemblance to a typical European capital and reflected few of the urban characteristics – such as anonymity and size – which Rousseau had so severely castigated in the previous century; in many ways it was still a small town and Kierkegaard was later to describe himself as 'a genius in a provincial town'.[3] Culturally it was very active, being particularly susceptible to the influence of larger European countries like Germany and France: the figure of Hegel dominated a good deal of university life and influenced the formulation of philosophical and theological ideas. German Romanticism was already a very powerful influence in Kierkegaard's formative years, as his early works clearly show. There was a very active theatre, giving German and French as well as Danish plays, while operatic performances were also frequent. In his youth Kierkegaard was to be an assiduous frequenter of both. If Copenhagen was a place where personal relations were still possible, it often witnessed intense quarrels and Kierkegaard himself in later life was to become disastrously involved in public controversy. However, the city was small enough to let people be known as individuals.

In 1821, at the age of eight, Søren was sent to the School of Civic Virtue (*Borgerdydsskolen*) run by a highly respected headmaster, Michael Nielsen, who was known as 'Professor Nielsen', having been given this honorary title by the University. As a schoolboy, Søren seems to have been of frail physique, being small and thin; his parents added to his difficulties by dressing him in unusual clothes, which made him the butt of his school-fellows; because of his apparently poverty-stricken appearance, he was frequently called 'choir-boy', a nickname which alternated with another, 'Søren Sock', an evident allusion to his father's trade. It would seem that he took his lessons very seriously, his father's influence making him treat them as an inescapable duty.[4] The general effect of all this was to make him feel different from other boys. Nevertheless, he was not content to suffer isolation and ridicule in a merely passive way, for he possessed a weapon which commanded considerable respect from both masters and boys – his sharp wit. In spite of his introspection, there was always an aggressive, polemical side to Kierkegaard's character, so that on occasion he could shine in company and obtain attention and admiration. He himself was later to speak of his 'dialectical' character, which prevented him from seeing things in simple terms. In his own words, he was in many ways a 'Janus Bifrons' who always looked in two different directions at the same time – inwards to his own melancholy inner life and outwards to the brighter world of social relations.

Although he was an assiduous pupil, he did not leave school with a very distinguished report; his headmaster wrote: 'He has a good intelligence, open for everything that promises unusual interest, but for a long time he was childish in a high degree and totally lacking in seriousness'. Mention is also made of his 'desire for freedom and independence, which also shows itself in his conduct by a good-natured, sometimes comical sauciness'.[5] In a later testimonial Nielsen was to refer to his 'industry, intelligence and intellectual grasp' as well as his 'far from common mastery of Latin'.

Kierkegaard was to sum up his childhood in the following terms: 'As a motto for my life in childhood I know nothing better than the words in Goethe's *Faust*:

> '*Halb Kinderspiel,*
> *Halb Gott im Herzen*'.[6]

In 1830, Kierkegaard entered the University, where he was to remain for ten years. He at first intended to study theology, in accordance with his father's wish. His initial progress was good, and he passed his first examinations *laudabilis prae ceteris*, in Danish, Greek, History and French, and obtained *laudabilis* in eight other subjects including Latin, Hebrew and German. He went on to do well in the next examination which concentrated on Latin and philosophical theory. Having completed these preliminary requirements, Kierkegaard then specialised in theology. It is, however, only from 1834 onwards that we have any detailed knowledge of his activities as a student, for it was in that year that he started his *Journals*. Although the early entries are related to his theological studies (there are several on predestination, the Atonement and other religious themes), his main interests seem to have been directed elsewhere – to literature and philosophy; consequently, he kept postponing the decision to prepare seriously for his theological examinations. A good deal of time seems to have been spent at the theatre and opera and he interested himself actively in student affairs. He gave a lecture on 'Our Journalistic Literature' to the Students' Union in November 1835, and T. H. Croxall has drawn attention to Kierkegaard's role in helping to inaugurate the University Musical Society.[7] Kierkegaard in these years was thus far from being a brooding lonely figure.

One of Kierkegaard's tutors was H. L. Martensen, who was only five years his senior, and had already been converted, by his sojourn in Germany, to enthusiastic support for the Hegelian philosophy; he was to attain a considerable academic reputation and eventually became Professor of Theology and, after Bishop Mynster's death, Primate of the Danish Church. He seems to have found Kierkegaard an intelligent, lively and very independent student who 'had his own ideas about how he should be taught'; 'he would have no fixed curriculum, but wanted me merely to talk to him and then discuss'. The tutor soon found that he had a devoted student who could at the same time irritate him with his 'sharp-witted banter'.

The widening of his intellectual and literary interests led Kierkegaard further away from theology and his original intention of entering the ministry of the Church. Moreover, he came to have very definite views about the nature of a work of art. One of the earliest entries in the *Journals* refers to his need to find the 'Archimedean point' of the work of art and the principle which makes it an 'organic whole'. A literary project of that period concerned the idea of a 'master-thief', who would be a sort of modern Robin Hood, an exceptional individual misunderstood by the world and using his activities as a means of protesting against the existing order of things; endowed with humour and a romantic appeal, such a man would be noteworthy above all for 'having lived for an idea'. 'He has tasted life's bitterness, and only because he lives for an idea can he carry on. . . . He often feels highly unfortunate in his position, because he is manifestly branded in many people's eyes. He feels himself *misunderstood* (which is the tragedy).'[8]

That this was no passing literary whim is revealed by Kierkegaard's subsequent interest in the myths of the Wandering Jew, Don Juan and Faust. Meanwhile, he was being increasingly drawn to the work of the German Romantics – Hoffmann, Tieck, Arnim, and others. A decisive intellectual 'discovery' of this period was undoubtedly that of the German philosopher J. G. Hamann, whose influence on Kierkegaard has already been stressed by Walter Lowrie.[9] In spite of his wide ranging interests he felt a growing need to find a guiding principle for his life. A letter written to (or intended for) his brother's friend, Peter Wilhelm Lund, on 1 June 1835, gives an interesting survey of his intellectual position. In spite of a short-lived enthusiasm for the natural sciences, he did not feel himself attracted to them and declared that he could not make them his chief study. 'Life has interested me most in virtue of reason and freedom, and to elucidate and solve the riddle of life has always been my desire'.[10] Likewise, theology presented him with considerable difficulties: he had been brought up in orthodoxy, but 'as soon as I began to think for myself, the tremendous colossus began to totter'. On the other hand, the broader attitude of rationalism also failed to satisfy him, for 'taken as a whole, it cuts a rather poor figure'; when it is pushed to the point of asking questions concerning man's inner life and his relation to God, it ceases to be rationalism and becomes a sort of hybrid or, in Kierkegaard's phrase, 'a Noah's Ark in which animals both clean and unclean lie down side by side'. Of one thing, however, he claims to be quite certain:

> I am supposed to read for a theological degree, an occupation which does not interest me at all and does not advance particularly quickly. I have always preferred a free, and perhaps too, a

somewhat indefinite study to the *table d'hôte* where one knows in advance the guests and menu for each day of the week.

Meanwhile, his personal life reflected the uncertainty that characterized his intellectual attitude. His depression was intensified by the deaths of his brother and sisters in the preceding year – deaths which seemed to justify his father's belief in the malediction threatening the family.* For a time it certainly seemed that the father would outlive all his children. Søren's tension and restlessness apparently gave his father some concern, for in the summer of 1835 he was sent on a holiday to the village of Gilleleie on the north coast of Sjaelland. Making a local inn his base, he made various excursions into the surrounding country-side and walked along the sand-dunes by the sea. He found this contact with nature and the sea a refreshing experience.

> In the midst of nature where man is free from the frequently oppressive air of life and can breathe more freely, the soul is readily open to every noble impression. . . . Here man steps forward as the lord of nature, but he also feels that there is something higher which manifests itself in nature and before which he must bow down; he feels the necessity of giving himself up to the power which directs all things.[11]

During this holiday he also felt the need to bring into his personal existence the steadfastness of purpose which he had been seeking in the intellectual sphere:

> What I really lack is to be clear in my mind *what I am to do*, not what I am to know, except in so far as a certain understanding must precede every action. The thing is to understand myself, to see what God really wishes *me* to do; the thing is to find a truth which is true *for me*, to find *the idea for which I can live and die.* . . . I certainly do not deny that I still recognize an *imperative of understanding* and that through it one can work upon men, but *it must be taken up into my life*, and that is what I now recognize as the most important thing.

The development and preservation of his individuality are associated with the need to identify himself with a personal truth. 'What is truth but to live for an idea?' He must direct his thoughts upon

> something that grows together with the deepest roots of my life, through which I am so to speak, grafted upon the divine, held fast to it, even though the whole world fell apart. . . . It is this divine side of man, his inward action which means everything, not a mass of information.

He goes on to say that he has 'searched with resignation for the principle of his life' and that 'one must know oneself before knowing

* They died at the following ages: Søren Michael, 13; Niels Andreas, 24; Karen Christine, 25; Nicoline Christine, 33; Petra Severine, 34, the last two dying in 1833–4; his mother died in 1834.

anything else'.[12] It is not until a man has truly understood himself
that he can give meaning to his existence.

Although these personal reflections indicate some of the main
themes of Kierkegaard's subsequent life and thought, his earnest
intentions seem to have been short-lived, for after his return from
Gilleleie, he was drawn once again into a life of distraction and
dissipation. He was frequently drunk, piled up debts and for a time
even thought of suicide.

It may have been during this period that there occurred 'the great
earthquake' which was to have such a profound effect upon his later
life.[13]

> Then it was that the great earthquake occurred, the terrible
> revolution which suddenly forced upon me a new and infallible
> law of interpretation of all the facts. Then I suspected that my
> father's great age was not a divine blessing but rather a curse; that
> the outstanding intellectual gifts of our family were only given to
> us in order that we should rend each other to pieces: then I felt
> the stillness of death grow around me when I saw in my father an
> unhappy man who was to outlive us all, a cross on the tomb of his
> hopes. There must be a guilt upon the whole family, the punish-
> ment of God must be on it; it was to disappear, wiped out by the
> powerful hand of God, obliterated like an unsuccessful attempt,
> and only at times did I find a little alleviation in the thought that
> my father had been allotted the heavy task of calming us with the
> consolation of religion.[14]

Kierkegaard himself does not give any further details of the event
itself, but it seems as though he unwittingly discovered some secret
which his father had kept hidden from his family and which also
explained his fits of gloom. Johannes Hohlenberg[15] calls attention
to a much later entry in the *Journals* which may well refer to the
same incident.

> An affair between a father and a son, where the son discovers all
> that lies behind, and yet dares not acknowledge it. The father is a
> worthy man, God-fearing and strict, only once in a tipsy condition,
> lets drop some words which awoke the most dreadful suspicions.
> Otherwise the son would not have got to know anything; and he
> never dares to ask his father or anyone else.

The precise manner of Kierkegaard's discovery – whether in fact his
father made an involuntary confession in a moment of intoxication
or whether he revealed his secret in some other way – is much less
important than its content and its effect upon Kierkegaard's life. In
spite of his father's indelible memory of how he cursed God in his
childhood, it is unlikely that the 'earthquake' refers to this incident;
more probable seems some kind of sexual incontinence. One can
imagine Kierkegaard's shock at learning that his serious, devout and
puritanical father had been guilty of sexual sin. To observant people
this could not have been a secret, for the birth of the first child five
months after the wedding must have caused some gossip at the time,

but as this had happened so many years before Søren's own birth, he could have remained unaware of it. In any case, it is possible that the father's secret involved some other sexual sin – a possible lapse before or outside marriage. A fuller discussion of the significance of this point will be reserved for our later account of Kierkegaard's melancholy, with which his father's guilt was evidently associated. For the moment it is sufficient to point out that if the earthquake actually occurred in 1835, as most biographers agree, it would certainly have added to Kierkegaard's demoralization, which had already come about for other reasons – for example, the deaths of his brothers, sisters and mother in the preceding years. As a result of these deaths, only two children, Søren and Peter, were left. The weakening of Søren's religious beliefs and his wayward life must have caused considerable concern to both father and brother, the latter of whom had already decided to follow a religious vocation; the Kierkegaard household may have witnessed at this time some heated discussions on religious issues, which perhaps explain Kierkegaard's reference to 'the remarkable intellectual powers through which the members of a family mutually torment one another'.

Whatever his religious position, there is no doubt that Kierke-gaard was intensely concerned with philosophical questions during this period and made his intellectual activity one of the principal aims of his life. The *Journals* contain an interesting entry which follows the account of the 'earthquake':

> Inwardly torn asunder as I was, without any expectation of leading a happy earthly life ('that I should prosper and live long in the land'), without hope of a happy and comfortable future – as it naturally springs from and lies in the historical continuity of family life – what wonder then that in desperate despair, I grasped at nought but the intellectual side of man and clung fast to it, so that the thought of my own considerable powers of mind was my only consolation, ideas my one joy, and mankind indifferent to me.[16]

To some extent the effect of all this was to reinforce the contra-dictions in his character, to make him feel that he had two selves – his 'real' self and his 'reflective' self:

> What I have often suffered from was that all the doubt, trouble, and anguish which my real self wanted to forget in order to achieve a view of life, my reflective self sought equally to impress and preserve, partly as a necessary, partly as an interesting stage, out of fear that I should have falsely ascribed a result to myself.[17]

At other times he had the feeling of possessing a double:

> Whenever I wish to say something, there is someone who says it at the same moment. It is as though I were a double thinker, and with my other self constantly stealing a march on me, or while I am standing and speaking, everyone believes it is another, so that

I can rightly ask the question which the bookseller Soldin asked his wife: 'Rebecca, is it I who am speaking?'[18]

The tension in the family home became so acute that for a time Kierkegaard moved into lodgings, and either there or elsewhere he became friendly with some leading writers and intellectuals, whose influence (either by attraction or repulsion) was added to more bookish sources. He encountered the famous Hans Christian Andersen, who was to be the target of his first major literary production, Jørgen Jørgensen, 'head clerk to the police court', according to Johannes Hohlenberg,[19] and apparently a frequent drinking companion and fellow-conversationalist, and especially Poul Martin Møller, an older man – cultivated and versatile who, in addition to being a professor of philosophy, was also a poet and novelist – to whom Kierkegaard later dedicated his *Concept of Dread* with the acknowledgement that he was 'the mighty trumpet of his awakening'. The *Concluding Unscientific Postscript* was also to contain an important reference to the influence of Møller who helped to detach Kierkegaard from Hegel and perhaps bring him back to Christianity.

That he needed some wise friend to guide him through these difficult years seems evident from his observations in the *Journals*, where he speaks not only of his sense of guilt but of the power of sin. Sin could at times seem to exercise an overwhelming fascination, especially for a man who was already oppressed by a sense of family guilt:

> A certain foreboding seems to go before everything which is to happen, but just as it can act as a deterrent, so too it can act as a temptation, awakening in man the thought that he is as it were predestined; he sees himself as led on to something as though by consequences which he cannot influence at all.[20]

An addition to the same entry points out that 'all sin begins with fear (just as fear of a disease makes one susceptible to it)'. Yet a further addition links up the theme with the memory of his father's moral and spiritual exhortations:

> It made a terrible impression upon me the first time I heard that the *indulgences* contained the statement that they remit *all sins*: '*etiam si matrem virginem violasset*'. I still remember the impression it made upon me when some years ago, filled with a youthful and romantic enthusiasm for a *master-thief*, I went so far as to say that it was only the misuse of powers, and that such a man might still be converted, and father said very solemnly: 'there are offences which one can only fight against with God's continual help'. I hurried down to my room and looked at myself in the glass – or when father said, as he often did, that it would be 'a good thing to have a venerable confessor to whom one could open one's heart'.[21]

He could not deny that the sinful possibilities of existence had a certain attraction: 'Yes, I believe I would give myself to Satan so that he might show me every abomination, every sin in its most frightful form – it is this inclination, this taste for the mystery of sin'.[22]

No doubt this explains one of the reasons for Kierkegaard's great interest in Faust at this time (a point to which we shall return);

> Faust did not want to know evil in order to rejoice that he was not so bad (only the bourgeois does that), but on the contrary he wants to feel all the sluices of sin opening within his own breast, the whole immense realm of possibilities; nothing else matters compared with that. He wants to be disappointed in his expectations.[23]

In spite of Poul Møller's efforts to draw him away from his dissipated life, Kierkegaard seems to have been in the grip of a growing despair and at times even thought of suicide:

> I have come just from a party where I was the moving spirit. Witticisms streamed from my mouth, everybody laughed and admired me – but I went out, and, yes, the dash should be as long as the radius of the earth's orbit – and wanted to shoot myself.[24]

His awareness of this duality of his nature led him to say: 'I am Janus Bifrons; I laugh with one face, I weep with another'.[25]

Even during this disturbed period he speaks of possible conversion, noting that it was 'a slow process' and quoting with approval Fr. Baader's remark that 'one must tread the same path backwards which one has previously trodden forwards'. Nevertheless, he did not envisage it as an immediate possibility: 'If it cannot come all at once, one may just as well wait and begin tomorrow and enjoy today'.[26] Direct intervention by his brother Peter seems to have provoked only irritation and resentment.[27] He also felt an increasing hostility to any social attitude claiming moral superiority, especially that of the bourgeois whose self-righteousness and complacency Kierkegaard was constantly to deride.

> Their ethics are a short summary of police ordinances; for them the most important thing is to be a useful member of the State, and to air their opinions in the club of an evening; they have never felt homesickness for something unknown and far away, nor the depth which consists of being nothing at all'.[28]

If he was still to be drawn to Christianity, it was probably with the help of a friend like Møller or an unorthodox humorist like Hamann, who preferred the anxious life of the individual to the smug comfort of a tidy philosophical 'system'.[29]

A casual visit in May 1837 was to have far-reaching consequences. At a time when he was feeling particularly unhappy, he went to see some friends called Rørdam; they had a daughter, Bolette, who was engaged to Peter Købke, a theological student-friend of Kierkegaard's. It was at this house that he encountered for the first time a young girl of fourteen and a half called Regine Olsen, the youngest daughter of a State Councillor and high official in the Ministry of Finance,[30] with whom he was to fall deeply in love. She is not specifically mentioned in Kierkegaard's own account of this visit, which shows, however, that he was strangely tormented by conflicting emotions.[31] (Regine Olsen was later to affirm that this particular entry in *The Journals* was prompted by their first meeting.)[32] His immediate reaction to her was to feel an increased sense of isolation, for a little later he wrote: 'I stand like a lonely pine-tree egoistically shut off, pointing to the skies and casting no shadow, and only the turtle-dove builds its nest in my branches'.[33] Certainly this sense of isolation did not strike Regine at that time, for she spoke of his volubility and brilliant wit. 'He made a strong impression on her. He talked incessantly, and his talk as it were welled forth and was captivating in a high degree'.[34]

It was only later – at the beginning of 1839 – that he met her again, although he thought of her often, occasionally saw her in the street, and constantly enquired about her. Meanwhile, his father agreed to pay off his son's considerable debts and, eventually, when Søren left home, granted him a regular allowance.[35] On his side Søren promised to do some regular work and took up an appointment as Latin master at his old school which was still under the headship of Michael Nielsen. Although he continued to read very widely and began to acquire a considerable library, his theological studies still hung fire. He suffered a severe blow on 13 March 1838 with the death of his 'confident', Poul Møller, who from his death-bed sent him a message: 'Tell little Kierkegaard to be careful not to make too great a plan of studies, for it did me much harm'.[36] Møller's dying message may have impelled Kierkegaard to think more seriously about his position. Be that as it may, two months later, on 19 May, his journal records a sudden religious experience:

May 19. *Half-past ten in the morning*. There is an indescribable joy which enkindles us as inexplicably as the apostle's outburst comes gratuitously: 'Rejoice, I say unto you, and again I say unto you rejoice'. – Not a joy over this or that but the soul's mighty song 'with tongue and mouth, from the bottom of the heart': 'I rejoice through my joy, in, at, with, over, by and with my joy – a heavenly refrain, as it were, suddenly breaks off our other song; a joy which cools and refreshes us like a breath of wind, a wave of air, from the trade wind which blows from the plains of Mamre to the everlasting habitations.[37]

Almost simultaneously there was an improvement in his relations with his father. Then suddenly in August the old man died, at the age of eighty-two.

My father died on Wednesday at 2 a.m. I had so very much wished that he might live a few years longer, and I look upon his death as the last sacrifice which he made to his love for me; for he did not die from me but *died for me* in order that if possible I might still turn into something. Of all that I have inherited from him, the recollection of him, his transfigured portrait . . . is dearest to me, and I will be careful to preserve it safely hidden from the world. . . . He was a 'faithful friend'.[38]

What his father had not been able to achieve in his life-time – to persuade his son to devote himself seriously to his theological studies – was now accomplished without effort. Kierkegaard's strong moral sense and his indissoluble bond with his dead father made him work assiduously for his final examinations which he took in 1840. His official request to the university to take the examination was accompanied by a very frank statement of his position: he admits that after an initial period of diligent attendance at lectures, he 'drifted further and further way from theology and eventually entered full sail into the study of philosophy which at that time was specially famous and brilliant among us. It soon became clear that I could satisfy neither the demands of theology nor my own desires. So I gave up theology altogether. I confess that had I not felt myself under an obligation through the death of my father, I should never have brought myself to resume those studies I had committed to oblivion, or turned my steps again in the way I had forsaken'. Since then, however, he had 'tried to swim back through the waves' and sincerely commended his studies to the 'venerable professors'.[39] He passed the examination without difficulty and thus brought to an end his ten-year existence as a 'perpetual student'.

Noises at dawn will bring
Freedom for some, but not this peace
No bird can contradict: passing,
    but is sufficient now
For something fulfilled this
                Hour,

    loved or endured.

                    Auden.

2 First Works

These student years had not been entirely unproductive from a literary point of view. Kierkegaard's very first publication seems to have been an anonymous article in the Copenhagen *Flyvende Post* entitled 'Also a defence of Woman's superior talents' – a reply to an earlier article, 'Woman's superior origin defended', written by a fellow-student. It was typical of Kierkegaard that he should have refused to accept the thesis of woman's superior (that is, spiritual) origin, for all his life he was to treat her as the embodiment of the immediate and sensuous, naturally hostile to the life of the spirit. This début, however, is more noteworthy for its attempted wit than for any seriously developed argument. More significant were the themes indicated in his *Journals*, though not as yet made the object of systematic treatment – the idea of the 'master-thief', and the legendary or mythical figures embodying characteristic attitudes towards existence: Don Juan, Faust and the Wandering Jew – 'the three great ideas which represent, as it were, life outside religion in its three-fold direction'.[1]

It is interesting to note that Poul Møller had also associated Kierkegaard himself with the character of the Wandering Jew, identifying his polemical attitude towards existence with the nihilistic attitude supposedly embodied in the legendary character. Møller himself had written part of a work on Ahasverus in which the character is represented as loving critical and polemical disputation for its own sake.[2] That this interest in legendary types was not transitory is proved by Kierkegaard's later work and especially by his detailed study of Don Juan. He was also amassing at this time a considerable literature on the Faust theme and he might have devoted himself to it had he not been anticipated by other scholars.[3] His student activities also involved him in some literary composition: in 1838, he wrote for the Students' Union a satirical play called *The Conflict between the Old and the New Soap Cellar*: *a heroic-patriotic-cosmopolitan-philanthropic-fatalistic drama in several scenes*.[4] His journalistic activity was resumed with the publication of four articles on political themes in the *Flyvende Post* of 1836. Like the earlier one, they were not very coherent, sacrificing serious argument to a display of wit. One contemporary journalist even wondered what their real subject was![5] As far as politics was concerned, Kierkegaard always remained a conservative, having little sympathy or respect for the contemporary liberal movement which he blamed for its lack of sincerity.

Much more interesting than these journalistic excursions was his first serious work, an extended review-article, entitled *From the Papers of One Still Living* which appeared on 7 September 1838 with the curious declaration that it was 'published against his will'. Although limited in size and content – its main theme is indicated by the sub-title 'About Andersen as a novelist with constant reference to his *Only a Fiddler*' – this early production is significant for a number of reasons. The strange title had an esoteric meaning understood only by the author himself, for it recalled his father's belief that the family was doomed to extinction. More important for the interpretation of the work was the statement that the author was publishing it 'against his will'. He may have been prompted to say this because of his attack upon Hans Christian Andersen the man, as well as Andersen the novelist; Kierkegaard implies that he is forced to adopt this hostile attitude against his own wishes, since his criticism involves a fundamental question of principle which goes beyond personal feelings. Nothing, in fact, could have been more different than the character and outlook of these two famous writers who may, at one time, have shared the same lodgings. Unlike his compatriot, Andersen had known a hard poverty-stricken childhood, which had marked his whole existence and his subsequent literary work. It is worth pointing out, however, that Kierkegaard's criticism was not directed against the author of the famous *Tales*, a genre which Kierkegaard himself readily accepted as valid, declaring on one occasion that the reading of fairy-tales was like taking a 'rejuvenating bath'.[6] Andersen the novelist, on the other hand, was criticized for his lack of depth and honesty, having allegedly projected into his fiction his own unworthy personal feelings. Again, it is important to recall that Kierkegaard was by no means opposed to the notion of an author drawing his inspiration from his own being (such indeed was the source of his own work); he would certainly have condemned literature which had a merely formal and aesthetic appeal; for, as we have seen, he was convinced that any worthwhile book had to be based on a valid 'idea' and animated by an organizing principle which gave it shape and substance: a life-view endowed a novel with its 'deeper unity' and 'centre of gravity' and so prevented it from being merely 'arbitrary' and 'purposeless'. Such a focal point was precisely what he found to be lacking in Andersen's novel, which, he alleged, was without serious content: it was quite unlike the true work of art which is 'the transubstantiation of experience' and the result of a genuinely creative activity, for 'genius is not a candle which is blown out by the wind, but a fire which the storm causes to flare up'.[7]

Andersen himself was not prepared to accept this violent attack without protest and he satirized Kierkegaard in his turn, depicting him as a parrot in *The Shoes of Fortune* and ridiculing his works in a play *En Comedie i det Grønne*. Kierkegaard was stung to make a reply in the form of an article, 'Just a Moment, Mr. Andersen', but it was never published because of Andersen's departure from Copenhagen.

Shortly after taking his final examinations, Kierkegaard went on a journey to Jutland to see his father's early home at Saeding. His diary of the journey gives a remarkably clear picture of his psychological state at that time. He was inwardly very divided, his moods alternating between joy and depression.

It is terrible the total spiritual barrenness from which I suffer at present, just because it is coupled with a consuming longing, with a spiritual passion – and yet it is so formless, that I do not even know what it is I lack.[8]

That his depression was due to the frustrations of idealistic impulses rather than to sheer emptiness is indicated by another jotting:

I am so dull and lacking in joy, that I not only have nothing which fills my soul, but I cannot conceive what *could* satisfy it – alas, not even the blessedness of Heaven.[9]

Although his depression was to make him write: *Nulla dies sine lacryma*, he was also aware of the resurgence of a spiritual need stimulated by contact with nature and the life of the villages and market-towns he visited. The heaths of Jutland were of all places most 'suited to develop the spirit powerfully'.[10] At times he grew enthusiastic over his experience of the poetic ideal, for 'the poetic is the divine woof in purely human existence' and 'the fibres through which the Godhead maintains existence,' even though the lot of the true poet is to be 'misunderstood, unheeded, criticized'.[11]

No doubt in his own life the poetic consciousness was not without its problems:

My misfortune, on the whole, is that during this time I was pregnant with ideas, I was frightened by the ideal, and so I gave birth to deformities, and reality does not correspond to my burning desires.[12]

During the journey, he was naturally not unmindful of his father.

I can never remember any change in my father and I shall now see the places where as a poor child he watched the flocks and for which, as a result of his description, I have felt such homesickness. . . . I learnt from him the meaning of fatherly love and so was given the same idea of divine fatherly love, the one unshakable thing in life, the true Archimedean point.[13]

Several observations testify to his continued interest in Regine, although a part of the diary containing references to her has unfortunately been lost. As we might expect, his reactions were by no means simple. While associating her with his potential idealism, he also feared the consequences:

May God grant that this should not be the case also with love; for I am seized by a secret dream lest I may have confused an ideal with a reality. God forbid! Until now that is not the case. But this dread makes me long to know the future, and yet fear it!

Shortly after his return to Copenhagen, he decided to woo her more assiduously. In his later years he was to give a long account of his courtship, the main points of which were subsequently confirmed by Regine herself. He relates that he had 'decided on her before his father's death'. One day, about a month after his return from

Jutland, he started from home with 'the firm intention of "deciding the matter" '. By chance he met her in the street, just outside her home.

> She said there was no-one at home. I was audacious enough to understand this as an invitation, as just the opportunity I wanted. I went up with her. There we stood alone in the sitting-room. She was a little uneasy. I begged her to play a little for me, as she did at other times. She did so, and that wouldn't satisfy me. Then suddenly I take her music-book, close it not without a certain vehemence, throw it down on the piano, and say, 'Oh, what do I care about music! It is you I want, I have wanted you for two years'. She remained silent. For the rest, I had done nothing to beguile her; I had even warned her against myself, against my melancholy. And when she spoke about a relationship to Schlegel I said, 'So let this relationship be a parenthesis, for anyway I have the first priority'. She was entirely silent. Finally, I went away, for I was in fear lest someone might have come and found us two together, and she so disturbed. I went directly up to the Councillor: I know that I was terribly concerned at having made so strong an impression upon her, as well as for the fear that in some way my visit might give occasion to misunderstanding, even to the point of hurting her reputation.

> The father said neither yes nor no, but nevertheless he was willing enough, as I could easily understand. I asked for an opportunity to talk with her. I got it for 10th September in the afternoon. I said not a single word to beguile her – she said, Yes.[14]

According to her own account, she hesitated for a short time, no doubt somewhat disconcerted by Kierkegaard's sudden declaration, but she then made up her mind and accepted him. Thereupon Kierkegaard made every effort to know the family, visiting them frequently and apparently dazzling them with his wit and intellectual brilliance.[15] Regine had several elder sisters and one brother, all of whom approved of the engagement. Nevertheless, immediately after he had taken the formal step of asking for her hand, he was overcome by doubt and felt that he had made a mistake.

In the meantime, he had begun to study at the Pastoral Seminary with the idea of qualifying for the priesthood. On 12 January 1841, he fulfilled one of his practical obligations which consisted of preaching a sermon. He chose as his text a passage from *Philippians* (I, 19–25): 'To me to live is Christ, to die is gain'.[16] His tutors were impressed by the serious content of his sermon, but thought that its severe description of the soul's struggles would prevent it from attracting the 'man in the pew'. Yet for the time being, the priest-hood remained a mere possibility for Kierkegaard, for he seems also to have had serious ideas of following an academic career. He was encouraged to do this by the knowledge that the professorship of philosophy at Copenhagen University was vacant. Accordingly, he began work on a thesis for the Master of Arts degree. As early as 1837 he had thought of a possible subject for his doctorate: 'The idea of satire among the ancients, the relations of the satirists to one another'.[17] Eventually, however, he settled on a rather different theme: 'About the concept of Irony with constant reference to Socrates'. It has been suggested[18] that Kierkegaard's interest in Socrates may have been partly due to the influence of his friend Poul Møller, whom he described as 'the fortunate lover of Greek literature, Homer's admirer, Socrates' intimate, Aristotle's interpreter',[19] as well as of the philosopher Hamann, to whom he had already been attracted. Although it was customary to write such theses in Latin, Kierkegaard was given special permission to submit it in Danish and have a *viva voce* examination in the same language. It was finally accepted on 16 July 1841, although some examiners, while approving its content, were critical of its unusual form.

The exact significance of this work has been the subject of considerable discussion,[20] some critics seeing it as very marginal to Kierkegaard's production as a whole and even at odds with it, others treating it as an important preliminary statement of his subsequent philosophical position. Perhaps too much attention has been devoted to the problem of its relationship with Hegel, for in spite of his frequent use of Hegelian terminology, Kierkegaard tends to treat Hegel as a historian of philosophy rather than as an ultimate philosophical authority. It is probably more rewarding to see the work in the light of the theme clearly enunciated in the title – irony and Socrates. It is to be noted that Kierkegaard's concern with these themes was at first linked up with his interest in the Faust legend. He saw both Socrates and Faust as remarkable examples of defiant individualism:

> Faust ought to be compared to Socrates, for just as Socrates represents the individual's emancipation from the State, Faust represents the individual, after the abolition of the Church, emancipated from its guidance and left to himself.[21]

A minor reason for his decision to concentrate on Socrates may have been the widespread attention already devoted to the Faust theme by contemporary scholars. As an academic study, the subject of Socrates may have seemed to offer more scope for original interpretation.

More important than the incidental reasons for Kierkegaard's choice of subject was the link between irony and his own temperament and interests. Unlike the genuinely tragic attitude which leads to the finality of death, or the madness which takes the individual beyond reality, irony permits the co-existence of contradictory aspirations and yet holds them together; it is an attribute which contemplates the tensions of existence while avoiding the need to take a decisive step to eliminate them. From the outset, however, Kierkegaard refuses to consider irony as a merely formal literary or intellectual problem, the ironical use of language being only a superficial aspect of a much deeper problem. Irony is seen as an existential problem, not as a merely intellectual or literary one. No doubt, with the clarification of his ideas, Kierkegaard's attitude towards Socrates underwent certain modifications, but he always held fast to this notion of the existential aspect of true irony. The contradictions involved in irony are not simply those between form and content, expression and real meaning; irony is rooted in the duality and ambiguity of experience, not in its mere mode of expression. In this respect, Kierkegaard was probably at one with the German Romantics, in spite of his severe criticism of their formulation and resolution of the problem.

Various entries in the *Journals* show that he had already begun to reflect on the implications of irony some years earlier. In 1837 he had observed:

> When the ironist laughs at the conceits of a humorist, it is like the vulture tearing at Prometheus' liver; for the humorist's conceits are not children of high spirits, but the sons of pain, and with every one of them goes a bit of his inmost viscera, and it is a poor ironist who needs the humorist's despairing depths. His laughter is often the grin of death.[22]

That irony originates in the contradictions of existence is a point to which Kierkegaard frequently returns. The very ambiguity of his own character – its dialectical, Janus-like nature – made him particularly aware of the relevance of irony to his own existence. As a melancholy man, he soon realized 'how close to one another are irony and melancholy'.[23] Yet irony is essentially a form of jest, a deliberate effort to avoid pain by laughing at it or by presenting it in the form of its opposite; in this way, the individual sets his suffering at a certain distance from himself by transforming it into an object of reflection and contemplation. Irony, therefore, reveals and at the same time conceals what it expresses. Kierkegaard describes this aspect of irony by comparing it to an echo:

> Yes, echo, you master of irony who parody all that is most noble and profound on earth: the word that created the world, by simply giving the outward form and not the fullness – yes, Echo, revenge all the sentimental rubbish which hides in woods and mountains, in church and theatre and which sometimes breaks loose there and deafens me to all else.[24]

Since the understanding of irony requires a certain intelligence and perspicacity, it will usually be beyond the comprehension of the masses. As Kierkegaard says elsewhere:

> To be ironical and in the majority is *eo ipso* a poor kind of irony. To be in the majority is the desire of all immediate people, but irony is suspicious in both directions, to the right and to the left. A really ironical person has therefore never been in the majority. That is the joker's position.[25]

Kierkegaard's own growing consciousness of the tension between the real and the ideal, between the earthly and the spiritual made him particularly sensitive to the implications of irony. At the same time he saw its dangers. Irony, as a refusal to act, can lead to an exaggerated absorption in a personal mood.

Irony is an abnormal growth; like the abnormally enlarged liver of the Strasbourg goose it ends by killing the individual.[26]

It can become a merely critical and negative principle which destroys the life of the spirit and 'paralyses' the individual with anxiety.[27]

These early reflections were to be given more systematic elaboration later on, as we shall see, and related to a definite philosophy of existence, but they already show that Kierkegaard's preoccupation with irony was no superficial or accidental one. In any case, his M.A. thesis gave him a very good opportunity of devoting further serious thought to the subject.

Without attempting to summarize the thesis itself, it may be helpful to indicate its general bearing upon Kierkegaard's philosophical development. His approach to the subject suggests that in spite of a certain indebtedness to Hegel and the German Romantics, the thesis is in fact a criticism of both, for the opposition to German Romanticism becomes quite explicit in the latter part of the work. In so far as Socrates was a master of irony – and this is the assumption behind Kierkegaard's entire argument – he was displaying a personal conviction and not a merely critical intellectual attitude. The method of assumed ignorance sought to achieve far more than the demolition of falsity and error, for it was intended to show how lived experience was at variance with a certain kind of philosophical knowledge. Yet if Socrates criticized his contemporaries, it was because he believed genuine ignorance to be an integral aspect of the human situation; he challenged the feasibility of establishing any positive truth and denied the possibility of the 'substantial life'. Socrates did not merely attack the so-called truths of others, but through his irony he sought to demonstrate the supremacy of the principle of 'negativity'. Since this negativity was absolute, it could properly be described as 'infinite negativity', which can be identified with the negative, ironical activity of a consciousness that constantly undermines objective truth. In limiting himself in this way, however, Socrates succeeded in relating the problem of truth to its proper source, the consciousness of the individual. Although Kierkegaard, at this particular stage of his career, was far from being ready to admit the validity of this negative irony, he considered that the Socratic attitude represented an important moment in the development of Western culture.

Later on Kierkegaard was to change his mind about his criticism of Socrates' negative irony, blaming his error on the influence of Hegel. He regretted having tried to show that it was 'an imperfection in Socrates that he had no eye for Totality, but numerically, saw only individuals'. Oh, what a Hegelian fool I was!'[28] Even so, Kierkegaard's ultimate emphasis upon the Christian Paradox compelled him to make reservations concerning the validity of a method which brought out the truth from within instead of allowing it to enter the individual from outside (God's grace); he was to see sin rather than ignorance as the decisive existential factor. Irony can never be more than a transitional stage of human existence, a stage at which the individual remains poised between mere possibilities instead of making a decisive acceptance of one of them. Kierkegaard, however, anticipates his later position in so far as he insists that irony moves between the ideal self and the empirical self, while decisively rejecting neither.

Kierkegaard concludes that, historically speaking, Socratic irony was a 'necessity' and not a mere 'possibility' or 'actuality', since it represented as it were a decisive moment in 'the development of world spirit', the embodiment of a fundamental 'idea' in its abstract, negative form. This becomes very clear when we observe Socrates' relentless opposition to the Sophists' specious claim to truth; his 'ignorance' effectively countered their 'knowledge' by convincingly demonstrating the emptiness of the latter. Indeed, Socrates abolished all false claims to the truth, so that even though he did not know the truth himself, he prepared the way for its eventual emergence: in Kierkegaard's words, 'he is the nothingness from which a beginning must be made'.[29] Socrates opened up the possibility of the ideal by showing that it could be approached only through infinite negativity.

In spite of his approval of the Romantic stress upon imagination and idealism, Kierkegaard is careful to point out the serious short-comings of Romanticism, which tends to dissolve into vaporous emotion. As he puts it in the *Journals*, it 'overflows all boundaries' and fails to distinguish good emotions from bad ones or the depen-dence of emotion itself on moral principles. Dreaming can be an unhealthy substitute for reality; in certain extreme cases – for example, when it is given infinite power – it may destroy reality altogether by passing over into madness or suicide. The 'infinite' longing of Romantic idealism may reduce finite reality to vanishing point. Lost in his subjective longing, and lacking both consistency and continuity, the Romantic is a being without roots, the helpless victim of his fleeting, ever-changing moods. Only great artists like Goethe and Shakespeare, concludes Kierkegaard, have been able to provide examples of 'mastered irony'; their creative genius has enabled them to control irony instead of being controlled by it. The typical Romantic writer, on the other hand, is the slave of the power which he is supposed to dominate, thus failing as both writer and person, even though the relationship between the two is never clearly defined. If, therefore, 'no authentic human life is possible without irony' which is a 'limiting' and 'chastening' influence and gives the soul a 'cleansing baptism', it is still important to remember that irony is only the 'negative way, not the truth itself'. Properly mastered irony fulfils its particular function by making the personal life capable of acquiring 'health and truth' and it does this by stressing the actuality of existence and the relevance of action. Yet all action and all actuality have to be sustained by a higher principle, so that irony becomes the starting-point for authentic existence, not its ultimate goal. In this respect, Kierkegaard recalls that the full implications of irony are incomprehensible without an examination of humour which, with its 'deeper scepticism', carries man forward to a higher ideal and takes him from the human to the religious plane of existence.

3 *Either/Or* (1843)

If Kierkegaard had hoped that the acceptance of his thesis in September 1841 would open up the possibility of an academic career, he was soon disappointed. In January of the following year, Rasmus Nielsen was invited to give some public lectures in philosophy and a few months later he was appointed to the vacant professorship. Meanwhile, still greater difficulties were involved in Kierkegaard's relationship with Regine. As we have already seen, his immediate reaction to the engagement was to believe that he had made a serious blunder. 'A penitent as I was, my *vita ante acta*, my melancholy, that was enough! I suffered indescribably in that period'.[1] At last, in August 1841, he decided to break off the engagement and he sent back the ring, with the following letter (which he subsequently reproduced in the episode 'Guilty? Not Guilty?' of *Stages on Life's Way*):

> Not to put often to the test a thing which must be done, and which when once it is done will supply the strength that is needed – so let it be done. Above all, forget him who writes this; forgive a man who, though he may be capable of something, is not capable of making a girl happy. To send a silk cord is in the East capital punishment for the receiver; to send a ring is here a sentence of death for him who sends it.[2]

Regine's immediate reaction was to rush round to Kierkegaard's room, but failing to find him there, she left him a letter in which she implored him 'in the name of Christ and his deceased father' not to abandon her. This made him realize that she must somehow be detached from him and made to give him up of her own accord. Regine's father at first attempted to placate Kierkegaard by offering never to set foot in his house after their marriage. Kierkegaard, however, remained adamant, although he agreed to see Regine again. When she asked him whether he ever intended to marry, he told her brutally: 'Well, in about ten years, when I have sown my wild oats, I must have a pretty young miss to rejuvenate me'.

'She said: "Forgive me for what I have done to you". I replied: "It is rather I that should pray for your forgiveness". She said: "Kiss me". That I did but without passion. Merciful God!'

> To get out of the situation as a scoundrel, a scoundrel of the first water, if possible, was the only thing there was to be done. So we separated. . . . I wrote a letter to the Councillor which was returned unopened. I passed the night weeping in my bed. But in the day-time I was as usual, more flippant and witty than usual – that was necessary.[3]

He was henceforth dead to all erotic love, even though he continued to love Regine in his own way, treating her as a muse inspiring his entire production. She was indeed 'the one unnamed, who one day shall be named, to whom all his work was dedicated'. At first Kierkegaard made desperate efforts to depict himself as a scoundrel and deceiver, in the hope that she would thereby reject him as unworthy of her affection. With the eventual publication of *Either/Or* he intended to reinforce this impression, for he sought to convince her that he was not only a scoundrel, but a potential seducer.

Almost immediately after the ending of his engagement he went to Berlin, mainly with the intention of attending lectures on philosophy and theology. He had great hopes of learning something important from the philosopher Schelling, who by this time had achieved a European reputation. Kierkegaard's hope of profiting from his attendance at Schelling's lectures may also have been based on that philosopher's avowed intention of refuting Hegel and of replacing his philosophy by something more positive and constructive. 'When he uttered the word "Reality" – in connection with the relation of philosophy to reality, then the foetus of thought leapt within me with joy as in Elizabeth'.[4] Nevertheless, Kierkegaard's hopes were soon dashed, for we find him commenting: 'Schelling drawls on quite intolerably'.[5] Dissatisfaction with the German philosopher helped to spur him on with his own book and he went home in March, so that he could complete it more quickly. It was published in February 1843. As the sub-title of the work, 'A Fragment of Life', indicates, *Either/Or* involved far more than his relationship with Regine; even though the work was intended for her, it dealt with his reactions to the whole cultural situation of his time.

In both size and subject-matter, *Either/Or* must certainly have astonished, fascinated and, at times, disconcerted his contemporaries as it has continued to affect successive generations of readers ever since. The title itself is a good indication of its ultimate emphasis and shows how far Kierkegaard's thought had already developed since the completion of his thesis. Far from remaining content with the uncommitted attitude of the ironist, he sought to induce his reader to choose a definite attitude towards life. To those who did not go further than the first volume, the nature of the choice might not have been very clear, for the subject-matter is extraordinarily varied in content and presentation: personal meditations, elaborate studies in musical, dramatic and literary criticism, lyrical effusions, odd essays on unhappiness and boredom, a strange 'Seducer's Diary', give an immediate impression of disparate material. In the second volume, however, with its elaborate treatises on marriage and the nature of the human personality, it becomes clear that we are being offered a genuine moral alternative to the point of view developed in the first part; the life of the 'natural' man – the 'aesthetic life', as Kierkegaard calls it – devoted solely to the pursuit of selfish enjoyment, often in extremely refined forms, gives way to the universal values embodied in marriage and the fulfilment of moral obligations. Whereas the aesthetic personality remains disastrously turned in upon itself, refusing to acknowledge any higher possibility to its existence than an absorption in its own feelings and emotions, the ethical individual identifies himself with the existence of his fellowmen, actively sharing in their moral needs and aspirations.

This fundamental antithesis sets the tone for Kierkegaard's entire literary and philosophical work, which gives prominence to the notion of existence as a choice between different possibilities: man cannot remain what he immediately is, but has to become a complete person moving on from a lower stage of existence to a higher one. Within the context of *Either/Or*, these stages are limited to two – the aesthetic and the ethical, but as Kierkegaard stressed later on, there was a still higher stage of existence which, though conflicting with the aesthetic stage, might also be at odds, in certain circumstances, with the ethical life itself. The importance of this third stage – the spiritual – was discreetly indicated by Kierkegaard himself not only with the 'sermon' of the Jutland priest on the subject of 'the edification implied in the thought that as against God we are always in the wrong', which constitutes the conclusion of *Either/Or*, but also with the publication in May of the same year (1843), under his own name, of two *Edifying Discourses* on specifically religious topics.

Either/Or was allegedly 'published' by a pseudonym (Victor Eremita, a name suggesting 'victorious seclusion')[6] who professed to be the mere editor of papers written by other pseudonymous authors, 'A', to whom the first volume is attributed (with Johannes, the author of 'The Seducer's Diary', a possible second author), and 'B', Judge William, the writer of the ethical essays. The attribution of subsequent literary and philosophical works to other pseudonymous authors, with Kierkegaard himself occasionally appearing as 'editor', has led to considerable discussion concerning the exact significance of the pseudonyms for the understanding of his work as a whole. No doubt the use of pseudonyms in *Either/Or*, like the deliberately disparate form of the work itself, owed something to the current vogue of Romantic mystification; it was important for a new author to capture his public and stimulate its curiosity by surrounding himself with an air of mystery. However, much more than this was involved. If we recall the basis of Kierkegaard's objection to Andersen's novel, the matter will perhaps become clearer. Like many other intelligent authors, Kierkegaard was anxious to make a distinction between his real self and his literary self. He considered this to be particularly important in the case of a didactic work which was not intended merely to amuse but to lead to decisive action. As we have seen, he always insisted that every work should have an 'Archimedean point' or governing principle, and in *Either/Or*, he wanted to make men aware of their real situation and in this way to persuade them to change the course of their lives. To do this he proposed to depict two kinds of existence – the 'aesthetic' existence which, in spite of its superficial attraction and beauty, was inadequate when taken by itself and was clearly lower than Kierkegaard's own personal life (in spite of what he wanted Regine to believe for a time); and the ethical existence with its noble idealism which Kierkegaard also felt to be beyond his reach, for he knew that he could not become the happy and dutiful husband and citizen portrayed in Judge William's essay on marriage. As he wrote in the *Journals*: 'I showed marriage as Or, but it was not my life's Or; I lie much further away from that Either. That Either means the enjoyment of life in its most unbridled sense'.[7]

By the use of pseudonyms, therefore, Kierkegaard was depicting certain aspects of existence which, though bearing some resemblance to the imaginative possibilities of his own being, never corresponded exactly to his true self and were, in any case, intended primarily as objective descriptions and typical examples of particular stages of human existence. As such, they had an absolute and 'ideal' quality lacking in any ordinary individual. In this way Kierkegaard was able to set a certain distance between himself and his work, and to consider it as something with which he was not personally identified in any narrow sense, but which none the less contained some of his deepest convictions about the meaning of human existence. In order to capture his readers' attention and persuade them of the seriousness of the problem, he portrayed characters who were far more consistent and absolute in their attitude than any real-life persons. At the same time these descriptions were the 'ideal' expression of genuine human feelings which would be familiar to readers of the book; *Either/Or* was a mirror in which they could see a pure reflection of their own personalities, and by seeing themselves in a new light, they would be induced (he hoped) to move from this lower stage of existence to a higher one. By means of his pseudonymous authorship Kierkegaard was also hoping to forestall the objection that he was parading before the public as a teacher who ought to be heeded in his own right; by concealing his identity, he made his own personal involvement or lack of it irrelevant to the validity of his message. Later on he was to give more careful thought to the idea of 'indirect communication' as a means of 'deceiving people into the truth'; he eventually realized that it was a method which had its dangers as well as its advantages, but from the outset he was concerned with the problem of making people aware of their true situation in a way that impelled them to personal decision; he felt that the best way of achieving this was for him to separate his personal existence from the work.

Undoubtedly, Kierkegaard's psychological make-up also lent itself to this use of pseudonyms, for he was fully aware of the coexistence of various 'selves' in his own personality, so that it was easy for him to delineate different imaginative possibilities of his personality without identifying himself completely with any of them. It was especially his introspective melancholy which impelled him to contemplate the various possibilities of his being:

For many years my melancholy has prevented me from being on terms of real intimacy with myself. In between my melancholy and myself lay a whole world of the imagination. That is, in part, what I rid myself of in the pseudonyms. A man with an unhappy home goes out as frequently as possible and would like to be entirely rid of his home, and in the same way my melancholy had kept me away from myself, while I discovered and practically lived through a whole world of the imagination. And like a man who has taken possession of a vast estate and is never tired of familiarizing himself with it – that is how I, in my melancholy, have behaved towards the possible.[8]

Because of this personal implication of his authorship Kierkegaard could treat his whole work as 'his education'. In challenging his readers to explore the various possibilities of their existence, Kierkegaard was also challenging himself to take an active attitude towards his own.

A characteristic feature of Kierkegaard's portrayal of the aesthetic life is already indicated in the *Diapsalmata* or aphorisms and observations with which the work begins.* The introspective nature of these reflections is emphasized by their being addressed *ad se ipsum* – 'to himself'. They also have some personal significance, for many of them are culled from Kierkegaard's *Journals* and are very relevant to his concern with the problem of his melancholy. However, they are here intended to have a wider significance, for they portray a typical aspect of Romantic *ennui*; the writer is imprisoned within his own consciousness, unable to break the grip of feelings which isolate him from other men and the world and make him the victim of his own unhappy mood.

The *Diapsalmata* indicate one of the main problems of the 'aesthetic' life: its failure to deal satisfactorily with the question of time. Although the aesthetic individual lives in one 'natural' dimension, in a single mood or colour, as he puts it himself (I, 28),[9] he can establish no genuine temporal continuity: his life lacks unity because it consists only of separate discrete moments, as he passes from one feeling to another without remaining permanently identified with any. Consequently, complaints about the meaningless of his existence form a characteristic refrain in these reflections. The diapsalmatist seems to exist in a void, with time flowing ceaselessly past him; on other occasions, time seems to have the opposite effect of standing still, 'and I with it' (I, 25). It is characteristic of the 'aesthetic' individual that he should seem incapable of development.

Yet the feeling of emptiness and purposelessness stops short of pure negation, the diapsalmatist's typical mood being one of boredom and melancholy; he knows that he cannot achieve the complete passivity of non-existence, for he is often beset by anxiety and frustrated longing. 'My eyes are sated and weary of everything and yet I hunger'[20]. The alternation of torpor and restlessness are a persistent feature of his existence.

In gifted individuals – in artists especially – this inner suffering may produce effects which delight other men. The very first entry insists upon this point and takes up a theme already stressed in the diary of the Jutland 'pilgrimage'[10], 'What is a poet? A poet is an unhappy being whose heart is torn by secret sufferings, but whose lips are so strangely formed that when the sighs and cries escape them, they sound like beautiful music' (I, 19). With 'suffering in his heart and music on his lips', he is destined to be 'misunderstood' by men and so thrust still further into his suffering. More clearly than in any other form of aesthetic existence, the poetic personality reveals an aspiration towards the ideal, a longing for perfection which cannot be satisfied in the everyday world. In this respect, it is apparent

* The word 'Diapsalmata' is intended to convey the idea of a 'refrain', for the writer is imprisoned in a single, repetitive mood. (Cf. a helpful note in I, 443).

that the poetic aspect of the aesthetic life, whatever its personal source, does contain a valuable and essential ingredient of every complete existence, for it shows that man is being constantly impelled towards an ideal which transcends merely animal satisfactions. For the most part, however, this is an urge which remains blind to its own real significance as long as it is separated from its proper existential context.

The aesthetic life tends to conceal its deepest need by expressing it in the form of its opposite. This is particularly the case with irony. Although at first sight the irony of *Either/Or* seems to resume the analysis of a theme already discussed in detail in the Master's thesis, its relevance is now restricted to a particular aspect of existence. It is not – like Socratic irony – a deliberate attempt to reach the ultimate basis of knowledge by the use of 'infinite negative subjectivity'; it is an activity which, by restricting itself to a single plane of experience, avoids the need to penetrate more deeply into the problem of existence: instead of engaging in action, the ironist delights in contemplating the absurdities and contradictions of a life limited to the enjoyment of the 'natural' self. Yet this conscious restriction of perspective is based on a powerful but unacknowledged need to express some kind of idealism. As Kierkegaard says of the diapsalmatist in the *Journals*: 'His enthusiasm is too vital, his sympathy too deep, his love too burning, his heart too warm, to be able to express itself otherwise than in the contrary.'[11]

It is interesting to note how, at the existential level, irony has a certain resemblance to poetry. Both are attitudes which refuse to allow the individual to commit himself to a serious identification with his inner self; they prevent him from penetrating deeply into the meaning of his existence, because they limit him to the enjoyment of mere 'aesthetic' possibility instead of impelling him to active decision. A victim of mood, the poetic and ironic individual remains on the surface of existence, suffering inwardly as a result of his frustrations, but refusing to move forward to open despair. No doubt this restless longing, this profound inner disquiet, could become the starting-point of a search for personal fulfilment, if its true meaning were acknowledged, but this would involve admitting the insufficiency of the aesthetic stage and a readiness to move on to a higher level of experience. This the aesthetic individual will not do, preferring to remain in a state of self-absorption. Consequently his personality is never complete and his life is never real, as he lives in a world of shadows and half-lights, finding a morbid pleasure in 'his dark imaginings, restless thoughts, dread presentiments and inexplicable anxieties.'

Were it not that the aesthete is dominated, in spite of his melancholy, by the need for enjoyment – even though it is of the limited possibilities of his restricted emotional moods – he might be driven to self-destruction. In fact, however, his anxious, ironical reflection gives him a kind of perverse satisfaction which he will not abandon. At the same time, he cannot avoid a grave distortion of personality. The diapsalmatist describes himself as being in some sense deformed: 'The disproportion in my build is that my forelegs are too short. Like the kangaroo, I have very short forelegs and tremendously long hindlegs' (I, 37). The ironist too is an ill-balanced being, for his mood is, as we have seen, an 'abnormal growth'.

The emotional implications of the aesthetic mood are elaborated in the curious essay on the 'Unhappiest Man', the man whose grave remains empty, perhaps because he never truly exists, or only in a way that leaves him poised between life and death: he is the victim of time, torn between memory and hope and yet accepting neither as he strives for the impossible ideal of living in both the past and the future. Other aspects of aesthetic melancholy are described in the portrayal of the 'brides of sorrow' in the 'Shadowgraphs'. These literary heroines – Marie Beaumarchais (of Goethe's *Clavigo*), Donna Elvira (of Mozart's *Don Giovanni*), Margaret (of Goethe's *Faust*) – are tormented by grief which, unlike the emotions of the diapsalmatist, has a specific cause, for they have been abandoned by the man they loved and trusted. Probably Kierkegaard created these portraits with Regine in mind, suggesting various reasons (none of them truly valid) for his abandonment of her. These grief-stricken women turn incessantly within the circle of their emotions, because they cannot be certain of the cause of their fate. Are they the victims of a deceiver, a mocker, or a demonic tempter?

In the preceding essay on 'The ancient tragical motive as reflected in the modern', Kierkegaard pushes his analysis of subjective emotion a stage further by asking whether subjectivity, when it is based on a noble motive, cannot be as genuinely tragic as the feelings described by the ancient Greek dramatists. This new dimension is added to the aesthetic life by the presence of hidden guilt. Whereas the guilt of ancient tragedy had been given an objective form in so far as the hero was punished by the gods or fate, the modern Antigone remains immured in a guilt associated with a secret which can never be revealed. Once again, through the character of Antigone, Kierkegaard is expressing his own situation, though in a very indirect and disguised way. He himself feels compelled to break off his engagement, because he possesses a secret (associated, like Antigone, with the memory of his father) which he cannot share with her or anyone else.[12] Nevertheless, it still remains possible for this attitude to be confined to the aesthetic sphere. Antigone is left alone with her secret and her pain, which co-exist with her equally strong love, and she is thus condemned to remain a victim of sorrow. Yet it is not quite certain that this attitude of unhappy secrecy was the only – or even the proper – one for her to have adopted. True, to have married with this secret unrevealed would have been tantamount to deceit (Kierkegaard himself was convinced that if he had revealed his secret to Regine, he would have made her as unhappy as himself). Even so, might it not be right for Antigone to attempt the impossible by trusting to faith instead of allowing herself to be destroyed by unhappy love? It is this element of uncertainty which limits the tragic possibilities (both literary and personal) of the situation.

Kierkegaard recognizes that melancholy is not the only possibility open to the aesthetic individual. The *ennui* of the aesthetic life can be dealt with in another way – by the activity of an intelligence that seeks to escape from the oppressive influence of boredom by constantly varying the mood. May not the bored man find satisfaction in cleverly exploiting the many possible variations of his mood, in extracting from each situation a kind of personal profit which will ward off the danger of monotony? The essay on 'The Rotation Method' insists that the truly aesthetic individual must not allow himself to be identified with a definite mood; he must free himself from any permanent dependence on the past or future, so that his greatest art is to forget; the event is forgotten, only the selfish emotion derived from it being remembered; no relationship in life – friendship, marriage, work – must be allowed to take hold of the personality, which has to remain open to ever-changing possibilities – to the 'rotation' which depends on the arbitrary will of the individual and not upon the objective demands of the situation. The aesthetic man thus avoids hope and regret, because he is constantly exploiting the possibilities of the accidental and shunning all involvement in the serious affairs of life.

The full implications of this reflective approach to the aesthetic stage of existence are brought out in 'The Seducer's Diary'. The figure of Johannes, the writer of the diary, cannot be separated from the earlier discussion of Don Juan, for Johannes, as his name implies, is intended to be a modern counterpart to the traditional Don Juan already discussed in the remarkable essay on musical aesthetics, 'The Immediate Stages of the Erotic or the Musical Erotic'. As is clear from the title, Kierkegaard seeks to show that the essence of eroticism can receive adequate artistic representation only through the medium of music. He does not treat the traditional Don Juan as a particular individual, but as the embodiment of a kind of primordial power, expressing the essence of the 'immediate sensual genius'. At this level, the term 'sensuality' or 'sensuousness' is not intended to carry any moral or immoral meaning, for it still is a primitive force which sweeps the individual along without any possibility of moral reflection or judgement. Don Juan, therefore, is an 'idea'; like Faust or the Wandering Jew who also express life outside the religious sphere, he epitomizes a vital impulse of the 'aesthetic' life. Kierkegaard considers that the direct emotional impact of music, its pure sensuousness, makes it especially appropriate to the artistic treatment of this subject. Opera, in particular, uses language in a way that lets the idea become explicit and yet keeps it strictly subordinated to the sensuousness of music. This perfect blending of medium and subject-matter in the musical representation of the Don Juan theme also had the good fortune to be treated by a really great composer – Mozart. *Don Giovanni* is, for Kierkegaard, not merely a classic, but a unique masterpiece in which all the potentialities of form and content are so completely realized that the feat can never be repeated or surpassed.

Perhaps this Mozartian Don Juan cannot be truly described as a 'seducer', because he is not an individual existing in his own right, but as a 'power that nothing can withstand'. The genuine seducer always uses reflection and cunning. 'This consciousness is lacking in Don Juan. Therefore, he does not seduce. He desires and this desire acts seductively'. That is why Mozart's Don Juan seems to suffuse the whole opera and gives life to the other characters who exist, so to speak, only derivatively. The entire work is the expression of the

joyous vitality and passion of eroticism, its meaning being determined by the total mood or 'idea' which it incarnates.

To this 'immediate' seducer represented by Mozart's Don Juan,
Kierkegaard opposes his second type, the 'reflective' seducer who is
not a quasi-symbolic figure expressing the spirit of sensuality, but a
particular individual who plans and struggles to overcome the
obstacles standing in the way of his desires and whose main concern
is to derive as much psychological pleasure as possible from the
breaking-down of his victim's resistance. Unlike the traditional
Don Juan, the interest of such a case is not in the number of victims
seduced, but in the manner of the seduction, the craftiness with
which the seducer carries out his task.

The last description of the 'aesthetic' life in *Either/Or* takes the
form of a diary and so recalls the introspective mood of the *Diapsalmata* with which the work opens. Johannes is a man who also lacks
a confidant; he remains imprisoned in his own personal reflection.
In the original draft of the 'Diary', Kierkegaard made a significant
comparison between Johannes and Narcissus, the man who fell in
love with his own reflection. For Johannes the dividing line between
reality and imagination has become blurred. Detaching himself
more and more from outward things in order to contemplate the
imaginative possibilities of his own being, he moves uncertainly
between the two worlds of fact and fantasy; as a seducer, he certainly
'has to do' with reality (since he needs a victim), but he does not
belong to it (I, 302). As he admits, he does not want Cordelia for her
own sake; he merely wishes to see whether 'one might be able to
poetize oneself out of a girl'; she is only a moment in the elaboration
of a subtle personal mood, the occasion for an experiment in poetic
reflection.

'The Seducer's Diary' constitutes a fitting conclusion to the
portrayal of the 'aesthetic' life, because its reflective quality allows
it to combine two elements whose interdependence has already been
indicated in the *Concept of Irony*, where Kierkegaard stresses the
connection between irony and poetry in German Romanticism. If
Johannes' poetic attitude is based ultimately on the desire to develop
the imaginative possibilities of the self, it is also bound up with the
process of constant reflection upon the 'unusual' and the 'interesting'. As a man who finds the normal social values of his environment
incompatible with his deepest needs, Johannes is prone to consider
as 'interesting' those situations (for example, his engagement to
Cordelia) in which 'natural appearance' is in contradiction with
inner reality. The interesting, therefore, does not depend mainly on
the objective meaning of any given situation, but on its ultimate
relationship with the secret impulses of his personality and especially
with the activity of his imagination; it is this strongly subjective
emphasis which is at the basis of Johannes' poetic and ironical
reflection. In this respect, the aestheticism of *Either/Or* culminates
in a highly 'Romantic' subjectivity of attitude which is at odds with
the demands of the real world, or rather, which tries to adapt the
real world to the demands of the inner life.

The perversity of such an attitude is particularly apparent in the
case of Johannes who treats other people as mere instruments in the

realization of his own possibilities. Cordelia is his 'handiwork', since he prepares her for the experience of love; but as soon as he has enjoyed the momentary satisfaction of seeing her as the embodiment of his own erotic desires – in other words, as soon as his 'ideal' self has obtained a fleeting experience of love's 'eternal longing' through the enjoyment of her feminine 'substance' – his interest ceases and he discards her for another victim through whom he hopes to find a repetition of the same experience. In spite of his 'aesthetic' claims, however, Johannes is not a genuine artist, for he produces nothing of permanent worth; he merely enjoys a momentary excitement through destroying the purity and innocence of another being. Nor does he achieve any genuine development of his own life, for he never escapes from his absorption in a single mood; the skilful and complicated variations of the 'how' of seduction cannot conceal the essentially repetitive nature of the experience and the seducer's inability to lift himself above the influence of a single static mood.

As in the case of the traditional Don Juan, though for totally different reasons, it may be doubted whether Johannes is a true 'seducer'. The basis of his eroticism remains obscure; but it seems to be of a curiously bloodless kind, and the physical culmination of his activities is almost an irrelevant afterthought. Perhaps he is 'too intellectually inclined to be a seducer in the ordinary sense'; he is an 'aesthete', who becomes so completely absorbed in the subtle imaginative and psychological implications of his adventure that he seems to lose sight of its physical termination. 'I do not care to possess in any external sense', he declares; he merely wishes to enjoy Cordelia 'in an artistic sense'. He gives the impression of being so cerebral in his attitude that he would almost be willing to dispense with its physical consequences. In other affairs too, he admits that he has often been satisfied to perceive a mere 'look' or 'gesture', for 'this is the most beautiful thing about the person concerned'. We are not dealing, it would seem, with (in Kierkegaard's words) a 'novel-hero', but 'a thinker accustomed to live in the world of abstraction', a man of mood rather than desire, an 'intriguing mind' whose constant habit of poetic reflection has undermined the sexual basis of his eroticism. At times Johannes' attitude gives the impression of a fundamental insufficiency and insecurity. It is as though he seeks to incorporate a woman's essence into himself in order to feel the reality of his own being; this curiously Narcissus-like figure needs a woman to infuse life into his self-image. Lacking real blood in his own veins, Johannes has to feed on a woman's living substance in order to sustain his poetic existence; as Kierkegaard observes in his notes, he is a vampire-like figure who 'sucks' in Cordelia's essence in order to remedy the deficiencies of his own debilitated life;[13] by 'constantly seeking his prey among young girls' he can experience a comforting, even exhilarating sense of 'rejuvenescence'.

Any potential idealism in Johannes can assume only a destructive, ironical form which will inevitably have grave psychological repercussions upon his personality. Like other aspects of the 'aesthetic' stage of existence, the attitude of seduction fails to give the individual any unity or continuity. He lives (like the bored man) only in the moment, flitting aimlessly from one episode to another without ever achieving any true personal identity. The result is ultimate psychological and moral bankruptcy. Unlike the traditional Don Juan, Johannes is not punished by the wrath of heaven, but by simply remaining what he is instead of becoming what existence would require of him – a complete individual developed and revealed in the light of the 'universal human'.

The second part of the work constitutes the 'Or' or true ethical alternative. It must be admitted that the first letter by the worthy Judge William could have been shortened to great advantage. The second letter, which deals with the 'equilibrium between the aesthetic and the ethical in the composition of personality', contains some remarkable pages and discusses themes which are central to Kierkegaard's whole view of man. The ethicist takes up the theme already implicit in the aesthetic stage but never brought out into the open – despair. As has already been suggested, the aesthetic life is based on an essential contradiction: it presupposes a contemplative, reflective attitude, an absorption in mood which, though aimed at selfish enjoyment, is ultimately stultifying and likely to produce only disastrous psychological consequences. When taken in isolation from the rest of the personality, the aesthetic life lacks continuity and has no guiding principle capable of linking up one moment with another, because it does not allow for any kind of personal progression, so stifling potential idealism.

The distinctive feature of the aesthetic life is its indecisiveness. To find fulfilment the individual would have to penetrate to a deeper level of experience and summon up his inner resources by choosing himself in absolute earnestness. What matters, in the first place, is not so much the nature of the choice as the fact that it has been made. Kierkegaard is not advocating a plunge into irrationalism; he is trying to lay down the conditions which must govern any kind of valid choice, whatever its specific object. Whereas the aesthete is dimly aware of his inner contradictions, he refuses to face up to them and will not attempt to break through the circle of his melancholy self-absorption by relating his being to a principle which has some kind of universal validity or objectivity. Unlike the aesthetic man, the moral individual makes a choice, and through the intensity of his existential effort, comes to realize that his true nature is bound up with his freedom. Freedom, therefore, is a primordial impulse preceding all specific decision, the expression of man's deepest self.

The essential point about existential choice is that it makes a man aware of himself as a true being, that is, as a being who does not live simply in the immediate moment but needs to choose himself in his 'eternal validity'. By identifying himself with his fellow-men through marriage, friendship, work and social relations, he is not simply affirming a kind of human solidarity, but putting his existence on a higher plane. As soon as he accepts the idea of duty and obligation, he is admitting his dependence on values which are greater than himself and yet intimately related to his own being; he is thus liberated from the hermetic attitude of the aestheticist.

The man who is still imprisoned in the aesthetic stage must be exhorted to despair; only then will he be able to escape from the limitations of his selfish attitude and move on to a higher plane of existence. Yet this new phase cannot be achieved by mere thought, but only by active choice and by inner decision. Moral values will emerge with the act of choice itself, for the individual will find that a new dimension has been added to his life by his experience of the 'universal-human'. Such a choice, however, does not mean the abolition of the aesthetic stage as such, but its transformation in the light of the higher stage of which it forms part. Beauty is certainly not to be despised, but, in Kierkegaard's view, it does not constitute a self-sufficient category, for it is only one aspect of a completely developed personality; true beauty is a quality of married love, not of the transient emotions of aesthetic love. The ethical element thus has the power to transfigure the aesthetic life by relating it to its higher possibilities.

In spite of the eulogy of moral values and the stress on personal choice, it becomes clear at the end of *Either/Or* that even the ethical stage is not complete in itself. The reference to 'absolute' and 'eternal' values inevitably leads on to a consideration of religious issues. Duty and obligation, for example, cannot be properly understood if they are separated from guilt and repentance. In comparison with the aesthetic, the ethical may certainly seem to be a higher phase of existence, but as is apparent from the homily of the Jutland priest at the end of the work ('as against God we are always in the wrong'), as well as from Judge William's comments upon the problem of the 'exception' towards the end of his reflections on the human personality, the ethical itself, when confronted with the still higher demands of the religious, may be involved in a tension and conflict which require it to be transcended.

4 The Exception

Either/Or was Kierkegaard's most extensive and detailed portrayal of the aesthetic life. Although he returned to the theme in later works, it never again attained the same prominence, for he tended to cast only a retrospective glance at a stage of existence that had been definitely superseded; he was to move on to moral and spiritual problems rather than remain tied to the life of the 'natural' man. His immediate intention, however, was to analyse in greater detail one of the central themes of the second part of *Either/Or* – the notion of 'despair'. In affirming that 'the choice of despair is "my self",'¹ and that the 'liberated spirit' of the true despairer 'will soar into the world of freedom' (II, 223), Judge William was raising an issue that was in need of further clarification. In particular, it was necessary to relate the existential aspects of despair to the other sides (especially the reflective) of the human personality. One particular question required close analysis: the connection of despair and doubt. To deal with this problem Kierkegaard set to work in 1842 on *Johannes Climacus or De Omnibus Dubitandum Est*. Unfortunately, it was left unfinished, because the events of his life (his broken engagement and subsequent relationship with Regine) made him turn to the composition of two other works, *Repetition* and *Fear and Trembling*, which were to have a more intimate and less general philosophical meaning. Nevertheless, *Johannes Climacus* remains an important fragment. From the very outset Kierkegaard considers doubt to be an issue of great personal significance and not a merely intellectual issue; once again he affirms the need to find a solid basis for his tormented existence.

Doubt is not (as with Descartes) a mere suspension of intellectual belief, but a deliberate act of *will* that refuses to believe; the doubter doubts because he chooses to do so.¹ This theme is given detailed elaboration in *Johannes Climacus*: 'Johannes Climacus saw that in doubt there must be an act of will; because otherwise doubting becomes identical with being uncertain'. Although there is a sense in which Cartesian doubt is also voluntary, it remains, in Kierkegaard's view, a purely intellectual attitude which does not reach right down to the deeper levels of personal experience; for Descartes doubt is a mere preliminary to the establishment of rational certainty. The famous Cartesian *Cogito ergo sum* is derived from the notion of doubt, but it remains a 'petrified proposition'. In a later work Kierkegaard reinforced this criticism by pointing out that 'for an abstract thinker to prove his existence by the fact that he thinks is a curious contradiction'.²

The particular danger of this method of intellectual doubt, according to Kierkegaard, is that people too readily assume that because one philosopher has doubted, he has doubted for all. This is no criticism of 'that honest, venerable and humble philosopher' (Descartes) who did 'what he said he did', but a rejection of those who merely apply his method in a superficial manner without going through genuine doubt themselves. To obtain an adequate conception of doubt it is necessary, in Kierkegaard's opinion, to go back to the Greek thinkers who were engaged in 'retiring' doubt as opposed to the 'inquiring' doubt of modern philosophers. Such doubt is the result of a strenuous effort which refuses to compromise with the comfortable attitude of dogmatic philosophers who put forward their opinions as absolute truths. 'Proficiency in doubt is not something achieved in a few weeks or days', but constitutes 'the task of a lifetime'.[3] As soon as doubt is located in the will, however, it cannot be overcome by mere knowledge, but only by another act of will, 'a free act'. In other words, it is necessary to transfer the whole question from the plane of reflection to that of *interest*. In this respect, Kierkegaard again insists upon the necessity of distinguishing between the 'reflective' and the 'real' self. Doubt cannot be resolved in intellectual terms, but only by the activity of a freedom that goes beyond mere reflection. Doubt, therefore, must always have a basis in the personality of the doubter; unlike mathematical and metaphysical questions, which remain impersonal and objective, existential doubt brings the individual into personal relationship with those philosophical problems which concern him. To think, therefore, is not to exist, because existence involves decision as well as thought: to exist is to choose, and to be free. Kierkegaard came to reject doubt as a possible starting-point for philosophy; perhaps 'wonder', as Plato suggested, was a more satisfactory one. In any case, the 'existential' and personal implications of philosophical questions always remained Kierkegaard's primary concern, and these were to be given a new emphasis by the events of his own life.

At first convinced that Regine would be permanently resentful towards him for the way in which he had treated her, he was astonished by her unexpected reaction. While he was at evensong in the Church of our Lady on Easter Day 1843, she nodded to him.

I do not know whether it was imploring or forgiving, but in any case full of affection. I chose a secluded spot, but she found me out. Would to God she had not done so. A year and a half's suffering wasted, all my tremendous efforts, and still she does not believe I deceived her, she believes in me.[4]

In spite of everything, Kierkegaard may have continued to hope that all was not lost. He himself said: 'Had I had faith I should have remained with Regine'.[5] For the time being he was detained in Copenhagen by the need to finish off his *Two Edifying Discourses*, but as soon as he had sent them to the printer, he left for Berlin once again. Everything, however, tended to remind him of Regine.

In Stralsund I almost went mad hearing a young girl playing the piano, among other things Weber's last waltz over and over again. It seems as though everything were intended to remind me of the past.[6]

He stopped work on *Johannes Climacus* and began another book on
a subject much closer to his immediate situation.

> I have begun a story called *Guilty – Not Guilty*; it could of course
> contain things which would astonish the world; for I have experi-
> enced more poetry in the last year and a half than all the novels
> put together.

This presumably was the episode of the same name later incorporated into the *Stages on Life's Way*; as a somewhat fictionalized
account of his engagement, it was as yet too intimately connected
with his recent experience to become the basis of a literary work. In
any case, the problem of his relationship with Regine had not been
finally resolved. As he observed,

> I do not wish my relation to her to be volatilized into poetry,
> it has quite a different reality. She has not become a fairy princess,
> and, if possible, she shall be my wife. Oh God, that was my one
> desire, and I have had to relinquish it.[7]

Clearly he still clung to the hope of marrying her, in spite of his
continued doubt and anguish.

He set to work frantically on two other books, which were
obviously inspired by his personal experience but through which he
also sought to raise questions of more general significance – *Repetition* and *Fear and Trembling*, which were eventually published on the
same day (16 October 1843) These works reflect the personal
preoccupation already apparent in the last section of *Either/Or*,
where the problem of 'the exception' is introduced into the account
of the ethical life; it is there suggested that the ethical, though higher
than the aesthetic, is not the ultimate stage of existence, since it cannot resolve exceptional cases. Kierkegaard clearly had himself in
mind when, in *Either/Or*, he spoke of the individual who was not
able to take up the universal into his own life; more especially, he
was thinking of his inability to become a married man. The problem
is given more explicit and careful consideration in *Repetition* and
Fear and Trembling. As we are here concerned with the general
implications of Kierkegaard's thought, it will not be necessary to
undertake a detailed autobiographical examination of these works
or to uncover the various mythical and symbolic disguises through
which the author seeks to hide his intimate feelings from the public
and yet reveal them to the only person who mattered – Regine. It
must be admitted that the role of the girl with whom the 'young man'
of the 'psychological experiment' falls in love is not presented in a
very flattering light, for she is said to be incapable – and perhaps
unworthy – of understanding the religious implications of his 'poetic'
nature; the blame for his unhappiness is thus laid upon her limitations rather than upon his. In this way, Kierkegaard himself was
obviously trying to overcome his own sense of inadequacy and fear
of marriage. Nevertheless, there was also an important moral
consideration: since marriage meant for him genuine reciprocal
trust and confidence, he could not enter it as long as he was weighed
down by the burden of his father's secret. Even so, he started work

on *Repetition* in the hope that, in spite of everything, some solution to the problem of his relations with Regine could be found and that she might finally be restored to him. He had already finished the first draft of the work when he received a terrible blow – he learnt that Regine had become engaged to a certain Fritz Schlegel. Realizing at last that his dream of eventual reunion was now quite impossible, he tore up the last pages of his work and substituted an ending that conformed more closely to the reality of his immediate situation. Instead of allowing his young hero to kill himself in despair, he made him confront the religious consequences of his final separation from the woman he loved.

The work is alleged to be 'a psychological experiment' written by Constantine Constantius,[8] who is concerned with the case of a young man who has fallen desperately in love with a beautiful girl but has encountered grave personal obstacles to the fulfilment of his desires. The structure of the book is determined by the attitude of these two characters, who represent Kierkegaard's own different selves – the reflective, rational being of Constantine and the poetic tormented 'young man'. The former takes a detached, almost impersonal view of the matter, seeing in the young man a case of more than unusual interest; the young man himself suffers all the agonies of a sensitive being divided by profound inner conflict.

The category of repetition is an important new concept in Kierkegaard's thought and is intended as a partial solution to the problem of despair discussed in existential terms in *Either/Or* and, more philosophically, in *Johannes Climacus*. At the personal level it was an expression of the hope that what could not be obtained in a worldly sense might be 'repeated' through an act of faith. By establishing a link between the decisive expression of freedom and the notion of deep personal concern, it also rejected the merely contemplative and reflective attitude of the 'aesthetic' stage of existence. At the same time repetition reaffirms Kierkegaard's interest in the problem of time already very evident at the aesthetic level, but now transposed into existential terms of greater significance.

In order to clarify the spiritual conception of repetition, Kierkegaard deliberately contrasts it with a more obvious and human expression of the idea: he makes this evident in an important entry in the *Journals* where he contrasts repetition as a conception which stresses the notion of variety and change expressed in behaviour and physical movement with repetition as a religious category which ignores the external aspects in favour of its spiritual expression and the change it brings to the inner life.

> Repetition is and remains a religious category. Constantine Constantius cannot, therefore, get any further. He is clever, ironical, combats the interesting, but does not notice that he himself is stuck in it. The first form of the interesting is to love change; the other is to desire the repetition, but in self-contentment and with no pain attached to it – Constantine therefore, is stranded on what he himself has discovered, and the young man goes further.[9]

The first part of the work describes the author's naïve and comical attempt to discover whether 'repetition' is possible in simple human terms: he tells how he returned to Berlin, in order to recapture the experience of the past, only to discover that 'there is no such thing as repetition'. (pp. 72–3). Ordinary human events and the feelings associated with them can never be repeated, because life is always moving forward, involving people and circumstances in ceaseless change; it is never possible to resurrect the past in terms of present experience. Superficially, however, it might seem feasible to seek a 'repetition' which would combine 'Being' and 'Flux', for the notion of repetition embraces both identity and change. If, therefore, we ignore the obvious misconception which seeks a simple repetition of events and feelings, it might be more rewarding to examine the implications of the notion for the development of man's inner life.

The question of repetition had already arisen in connection with the aesthetic life portrayed in *Either/Or*, where it had been characterized either by the monotony of melancholy or by ceaseless efforts to bring variety to a single mood. The characteristic attitude of the aesthetic man is his preoccupation with an enjoyment that causes him to flit from one pleasure to another, so that his entire existence consists of a series of moments which express 'repetition' of a particularly superficial kind; the concern with variety, however skilfully disguised, is simply a ceaseless repetition of the same unprogressive psychological attitude. It is this very lack of personal development which ultimately ends in despair, for fundamentally the aesthetic individual is running counter to the true possibilities of human existence. In spite of all his shrewdness and cunning – for example, as described in the 'Rotation Method' – he cannot escape from the consequences of his restricted position. Such 'freedom' as he exercises is of a purely mental or psychological kind, a playing with possibilities which make no serious impact upon his inner life; it is an attitude based on quantity rather than quality. The reason for this is quite simple; his freedom is restricted to the finite and temporal and shuns any effort to express the deeper levels of experience where more stable and permanent values might be found.

Repetition will occur only when existence has been raised to a higher plane and when the transitory experiences of the aesthetic life are either replaced by or integrated into a personal attitude of more general validity. Such, at first sight, seems to be the case with the moral stage of existence described in *Either/Or*; the ethical individual is able to escape from the temporal fragmentation of his life, because his inner being is identified with universal moral principles and so achieves genuine personal continuity; he no longer depends on moments of fleeting and precarious pleasure, but possesses a self whose constancy overcomes the limitations of time. In other words, it is only through the experience of moral freedom that the inadequacy of the aesthetic life can be effectively avoided.

Nevertheless, it may be doubted whether this ethical conception of existence is capable of achieving a 'repetition' in the true sense of the term; the individual finds continuity and identity, but he does not, strictly speaking, receive anything back. It is true that the

Stoics seemed to obtain some kind of moral repetition, since they turned away from the external world in order to achieve a constant and unshakable inner unity; but Kierkegaard points out that the Stoic attitude maintains inner unity only at the cost of limiting the expression of freedom. Admittedly, as long as he remains involved with ethical values, the young man of *Repetition* may still hope to achieve some kind of human repetition; like Kierkegaard himself, he may still seek to 'repeat' his engagement and marry the girl he loves. But as soon as this ethical possibility is removed, no simple solution remains open to him: it is necessary for him to seek the recovery of his true self at a still higher plane of experience. He has to acknowledge that far more is involved than a merely rational human happiness based on either personal or moral principles. What the individual gains through repetition may be precisely the opposite – the loss of personal happiness, as was the case with Kierkegaard when he lost Regine. Henceforth, he has to seek a 'genuine enrichment' and a further development of his inner being. What cannot be resolved in human terms has to be transferred to the domain of the spiritual. Henceforth 'eternity is the true repetition'.

The introduction of the 'transcendent' and 'eternal' into the notion of repetition makes it essentially forward-looking and thereby distinguishes it from the Platonic idea of recollection; the Greek view does not allow for any genuinely new spiritual principle to emerge, since it merely brings out what is already immanent in the individual. Repetition, therefore, looks forward to new faith rather than backwards to what already exists. In Kierkegaard's phraseology, it is not possible to achieve repetition by the philosophical principle of 'mediation' which, in the Hegelian system, presupposes the synthesis of possibility and actuality in the form of necessity, but only by the radical expression of a freedom which requires a leap (and not a simple transition) to a higher plane of being. Once again we see how repetition is attained through transcendence rather than immanence; it does not come into being by means of a gradual movement from one state to another, but only by a definite process of *becoming*. 'In the sphere of logic transition is mute, in the sphere of freedom it becomes'.[10] Becoming, therefore, is inseparable from the idea of personal possibility, from a decisive choice and a qualitative transformation of inner being.

It is important to indicate the break not only between repetition and the aesthetic life, but also between repetition and the whole notion of metaphysics as understood by traditional philosophy. In this respect the argument of *Repetition* takes up the points already made about doubt and despair in *Johannes Climacus*, but the problem is made particularly acute by the exceptional nature of the young man whose dilemma cannot be overcome by the use of the general categories applicable to the understanding of humanity and its relationship with the world: he seeks an 'interest' which will give a personal meaning to his own particular existence and take him beyond the abstract categories of metaphysics. Even ethical principles, as we have seen, are not relevant to his case. He is in search of something that is genuinely new, and capable of lifting him above the conflicts and divisions associated with his struggle to resolve his problem in human terms and yet of allowing him to be *himself*.

Although Kierkegaard's own explanation of the meaning of 'repetition', as well as Constantine Constantius' remarks in certain sections of the work itself, point to the broader significance of the notion, it can acquire reality only when it is expressed in the existence of the living individual. The 'young man' sees repetition as a means of overcoming his personal problem in religious terms: his love for the girl has made him aware of a new possibility of his being, of a poetic ideal which threatenes to conflict with the moral and rational fulfilment of himself in marriage. He is torn by inner conflict, because he gradually realizes that he is an 'exception'. The act of falling in love has awakened him to a possibility which had until then been completely dormant: he is now drawn to a mode of existence which will involve values transcending and conflicting with the demands of the ethical as well as of the aesthetic life. The doubts expressed at the end of *Either/Or* about the universal validity of the ethical stage are now given much more explicit and intense formulation. At first the young man remains confused and unhappy and abandons himself to a mood that is reminiscent of the attitude of the diapsalmatist in *Either/Or*: 'I loathe existence: it is without savour, lacking salt and sense . . . I stick my finger into existence; it smells of nothing'. Gradually, however, he is overwhelmed by more powerful, tormenting emotions which make it impossible for him to return to his earlier innocence and yet prevent him from having a clear perception of the path he is to follow.

A new factor is introduced into his life when his contradictions begin to revolve about the notion of guilt. Is he guilty or not in his behaviour towards the girl? Doubt about the possibility of marriage, though associated with the thought that he has 'acted correctly' in refusing to be the girl's husband, continues to worry him. Even though the girl's reality is reduced to 'a shadow which runs alongside my proper spiritual reality, a shadow which at one moment would make me laugh, at another would intrude disturbingly into my existence', he cannot free himself from his love. One part of his nature still wishes for marriage in spite of all the obstacles, and he wonders whether his doubt and guilt can be overcome by an act of faith which will bring about a genuine 'repetition' in the form of marriage.

One interesting religious consequence of his situation is that the young man begins to reflect increasingly on the Biblical figure of Job, whose position resembles his own in several ways. In the first place, Job was a man who knew the 'passion of pain', because he became absorbed in an 'idea' which took him beyond the sympathy and understanding of his fellow-men. Like the young man too, he was aware of himself as an exception, an individual whose misfortune, far from making him rebel against God, induced him to treat his suffering as a test to be endured. The whole thing, affirms the young man, was 'a trial of probation'. He was grappling with the values which had meaning only for his own exceptional personal experience. Job was alone in the world, because he had to confront God in the solitude of his individual being. He was existing, therefore, in relation to a 'transcendent' reality which removed him from the domain of the aesthetic, the ethical and the dogmatic: his conduct and attitude could not be judged in terms of objective, universal principles, from whatever source they were drawn. This does not mean that Job was actually a 'hero of faith'; he was simply an exceptional individual experiencing a 'trial which related to eternity' (p. 131).

Job's problem was not resolved in a normal way. He had to rely, as it were, on God's initiative and await the 'thunderstorm' through which God spoke to him. Reproved in the eyes of men, Job was none the less vindicated by God, though perhaps in a way that others would not understand but which Job himself accepted with the consolation that he was 'blessed by God and had known true repetition by receiving everything double'. Just as Job had patiently to wait for God's voice, so must the young man await his 'repetition' through which, in spite of seemingly overwhelming obstacles, he may also get back everything, including the girl he loves. (Such, for a time, was Kierkegaard's own hope in relation to Regine.) Perhaps, after all, he is meant to be a husband, even though it is an experience which will 'crush him completely'. The rational Constantine Constantius considers that the young man's hope is ill-founded, since he is a poet in love with an ideal that makes him unfitted for marriage. Yet Constantine is only the voice of reason, not of faith, and through faith the individual may achieve an experience unobtainable by ordinary human means.

As in the case of Kierkegaard himself, the young man's dilemma is resolved for him in an unexpected way when he suddenly learns of the girl's marriage to another. Freed from the necessity of initiating any action, he insists that he is 'again himself', that he has the 'repetition' he has sought for so long. He now realizes, however, that repetition cannot mean the restoration of some finite condition or getting back everything double in a worldly sense and, in this respect, Job's example was misleading. Only spiritual repetition is possible, although in temporal life it is never so perfect as in eternity, which is the true repetition.

Yet the conclusion of *Repetition* makes it clear that the young man is as yet only on the confines of faith: if he is an exception, it is as a poet, who merely 'represents the transition to the more properly aristocratic exceptions, namely, the religious exceptions' (p. 154). A poet's life begins in conflict, as has already been made clear at the aesthetic stage, and it helps him to realize that his own consciousness cannot remain immersed in immediacy but must take the form of a 'consciousness raised to the second power'. He is aware of his higher spiritual need, though as yet it is not clearly formulated. The poetic young man has been made aware of the 'idea', but he is not 'thoroughly clear about what he has done or about what he truly can become'. Yet he still remains an exceptional being, for something which in others might have been merely commonplace (inner doubts about the possibility of marriage) 'assumed in his case the proportions of a cosmic event' (p. 159).

The problem of the exception could obviously not be left at the point reached by the 'young man'. If the freedom of repetition was the 'breaking wave which hurled him up above the stars' (p. 149), the precise meaning of this adventure was not yet clear. Although the new possibilities of his existence separated him from his previous life by involving him in a new and shattering experience – that of eternity – the particular path he was to follow remained as yet unknown. The work which accompanied *Repetition* – *Fear and Trembling* – attempted to draw out the consequences of this momentous encounter with eternity.

Kierkegaard himself always thought highly of the book.

> Once I am dead, *Fear and Trembling* alone will be enough to immortalize my name. It will be read and translated into foreign languages. People will shudder at the terrible pathos which the book contains.[11]

As in the case of *Repetition*, Kierkegaard was still preoccupied with his personal problem while seeking to give it more general significance. '*Fear and Trembling* reproduced my own life'. Yet he hoped that it would provide insight into the lives of others who were struggling with the problem of religious faith.*

In spite of the close personal link between the two works there is an important difference of literary form. Whereas the main character of *Repetition* was the poetic young man whose suffering eventually led him to meditate on the case of Job, *Fear and Trembling* gives prominence at the very outset to the biblical figure of Abraham – of the Abraham whose faith made him ready to sacrifice his only son, Isaac. Instead of being gradually led to a consideration of a biblical character, the reader is immediately confronted with one who was deeply involved in the demands of religious faith. Although there is a sense in which Abraham, like Job, is also on trial, his case is not quite the same, for his children were not taken away from him by some inscrutable external power; he was called upon to sacrifice his only son by his own act. The collision with ethical values was much more violent and the experience of faith 'by virtue of the absurd' much more anguishing, for he could not escape from a sense of personal responsibility. (That Kierkegaard's meditation upon Abraham was intended to be relevant to his own situation is also clear, for he too saw himself as a man impelled to sacrifice his only love to a higher religious demand; the objective manner of presentation, however, makes it clear that he considered his own case in the light of a much greater and nobler one). Whereas *Repetition* had left the problem of inner conflict without a definite conclusion, for the young man had simply attained some conception of the possibility – rather than the reality – of a religious ideal, *Fear and Trembling* faces the problem of faith in a much more explicit way. Moreover, the attribution of this work to a new pseudonym, Johannes de Silentio, who writes from the 'silence' of his inner life,

---

* Nevertheless, the attribution of the work to the pseudonym 'Johannes de Silentio' shows that it was intended only for the 'serious observer who himself disposes of religious presuppositions, the serious observer to whom it is possible to make oneself intelligible at a distance, and to whom one can talk in silence'.[12]

and the use of the motto drawn from Hamann – 'What Tarquinius Superbus said in his garden by means of the poppy-heads, was understood by the son, but not by the slave' – show that Kierkegaard is taking the problem of the exception on to a more remote and unfamiliar plane of experience.

A sacrifice like Abraham's raises in a very acute form the question of putting aside the fulfilment of moral obligations for the sake of some higher ideal. With religious faith of this kind we move from the safe ground of universal values to the paradox and uncertainty of individual faith. Judged by moral standards, Abraham was a potential murderer, and yet, when he is seen as a truly religious figure, he becomes a man of faith. The religious individual who acts 'by virtue of the absurd' is to be sharply distinguished from the tragic hero, because the tragic hero is making a moral sacrifice which, in spite of the personal pain it involves, can be rationally justified by reference to some higher good; the 'knight of faith', on the other hand, knows no such justification, for he cannot relate his situation to the realm of universal values. If he is great, it is by virtue of some purely personal virtue which defies rational explanation and separates him from his fellow-men: he is involved in a particular relationship with the divine. Abraham is confronted with the paradox that accompanies the individual's efforts to express some absolute value in his existence. 'Faith is this paradox, that inwardness is superior to the external' (p. 88). In faith the individual attains a new 'immediacy', not, of course, the immediacy of the aesthetic life, but the immediacy of religious faith, and this transcends the universal since it puts him into direct relationship with the absolute. The knight of faith is cut off from others, for he 'depends entirely and absolutely on himself' (p. 103); his 'passionate concentration' and 'energetic consciousness' keep him constantly in suspense; he knows that his strenuous efforts to find spiritual fulfilment involve him in an 'absolute relationship with the absolute'. This does not mean, however, that the man of faith is blind to the importance of morality or the value of ordinary human feelings; he is just as sincerely attached to them as any other man, but he knows that these are not the ultimate end of existence, that faith may make him renounce them for the sake of some higher ideal. His anguish and suffering, however, are increased by his full consciousness of what he is giving up for the sake of the absolute.

Yet the paradox of faith also isolates him from his fellow-men; he cannot 'possibly make himself intelligible to anyone' (p. 92). This isolation raises a serious problem – the problem of whether he can be ethically justified in maintaining silence in the presence of his fellow-men. Once again, Kierkegaard touches upon his own personal dilemma. Was he truly justified in refusing to reveal his secret to Regine? That his silence brought suffering to her was undeniable, but was it absolutely certain that inner truth had to remain hidden in this way? Admittedly, inwardness is an indispensable condition of faith, but is there not also a self-absorbed inwardness which is demoniacal rather than religious?

Silence may be due to a number of reasons, as Kierkegaard tries to show by the use of stories and myths. He first mentions Aristotle's story of the bridegroom who, when he was told by the augurs that his marriage would end in personal disaster, suddenly abandoned his bride at the very moment of the wedding ceremony. The problem is: was it such a man's duty to explain himself? Kierkegaard suggests three possibilities: firstly, he could have remained silent and gone on with the ceremony, but this would have been wrong because, even though the augurs specified that the disaster would fall upon him alone, he would inevitably have involved his bride in his own guilt and suffering; secondly, he could have remained silent and refused to go on with the marriage, but this would have led to a 'mystification in which he destroyed himself in relation to her' and also brought suffering to the girl; lastly, he could have spoken out and explained the reasons for his action. This would seem to be what ethics required of him, and in Greece it would have created no problem, because the augurs' prophecies were intelligible to everyone. A different situation would have arisen if the divine prohibition had been communicated to the bridegroom in a purely private manner, for this would have brought him into the presence of a paradox which might well have prevented him from speaking; his silence would then have been rooted in something deeper than ethical obligation, for it would have involved his desire to enter into an absolute relationship with the absolute.

Kierkegaard goes on to give further illustrations of the theme in the stories of Agnes and the Merman, with its corollary of demonic silence, of Sarah and Tobias (yet another example of defiant and possibly demonic silence) and of Faust who concealed his doubt. These are obviously symbolic accounts of Kierkegaard's own dilemma in relation to Regine: he continued to be tormented by the demonic possibility inherent in his refusal to explain himself openly to her. He makes it clear that there is a great difference between the demonic silence of the individual who is merely prevented from speaking by some purely psychological motive and the man of faith who maintains silence because of his relationship with the absolute; inhibition has to be sharply distinguished from faith. In the end, we are brought back to the example of Abraham, who is neither an 'aesthetic hero' nor a 'real tragic hero' who 'sacrifices himself and everything he possesses to the universal'. Because there is no objective universal principle by which Abraham can justify his behaviour, he is plunged into anguish and suffering and the 'terrible responsibility of solitude'. Nevertheless, he has one supreme consolation – faith in God who, he believes, 'will give him a new Isaac by virtue of the absurd'. What then, are we to conclude from this examination of Abraham's case? Simply this: either there exists this paradox, that the Individual as the Individual stands in an absolute relationship to the Absolute, or Abraham is lost.

5 The Secret

As Kierkegaard approached the threshold of religious faith, he was forced to ponder yet again the implications of his personal decision. That he felt a recurrent need to return to the thought of his broken engagement is shown by the inclusion in *Stages on Life's Way* (published in 1845) of the episode 'Guilty? Not Guilty?' through which Kierkegaard sought to give a last public, though disguised, account of his relations with Regine and their personal consequences. In considering this episode apart from the rest of the book, we shall not be seriously distorting its meaning, since it was first conceived as a separate work which Kierkegaard thought of publishing under the title of *Right Hand and Left Hand*. In any case, it has a direct bearing upon the personal themes already discussed in the earlier works.

The form of 'Guilty? Not Guilty?' recalls that of *Repetition*, in so far as we are allegedly dealing with a 'psychological experiment' carried out by Frater Taciturnus, who, like his predecessor Constantine Constantius, is a rational, detached observer interested in the case of a poetic young man – Quidam ('A certain one') – who is struggling to fulfil a personal ideal in spite of his involvement in an unhappy love-affair: after falling desperately in love with a girl to whom he becomes engaged, he is wracked by doubt and suffering. As with the 'young man' of *Repetition*, Quidam has to face the inhibiting effect of his 'melancholy' which is once again associated with the idea of a terrible secret.

Before discussing in greater detail the problem of Kierkegaard's own secret, to which the diary is obviously referring, it may be helpful to consider Quidam's personal dilemma in the context of the 'Diary' as a whole. For this purpose, we may defer for the time being an examination of Frater Taciturnus' remarks, which are intended to be an impersonal analysis of the problem and an interpretation of its general meaning. Quidam himself speaks of his melancholy and his inability to disguise it. In spite of the absolute, exclusive nature of his love – 'either her or nothing' – he cannot overcome the ambivalent feelings associated with his 'morbid reserve'.[1] These not only cut him off from the one he loves so intensely, but also impel him to present himself to her as other than he really is – a scoundrel instead of a devoted lover. At the same time, he is aware of their profound incompatibility of character: whereas she is frivolous, child-like and without 'religious postulates', he is consumed by a spiritual hunger, as he yearns for the eternal through a 'lonely under-standing with God'.[2] Yet like the young man of the earlier work, Quidam still seeks a 'repetition' in Job-like terms, hoping that he will achieve marriage in spite of his 'morbid reserve'. Although he occasionally falls into the *ennui* of the aesthetic mood, as he experiences the emptiness already described by the diapsalmatist of *Either/Or*, he concentrates for the most part on a theme that had appeared at the end of *Repetition* – the question of his guilt and his

D

need for repentance; he comes to interpret his suffering as a punishment for what he has done.

At one point, Quidam makes a passing reference to a matter of
decisive significance for his whole attitude: he says that he is 'bound
by a dead man – his father'. Although the father is only briefly
mentioned in the main part of the 'Diary', he reappears frequently
in the six strange episodes which are inserted in the midst of Quidam's
self-analysis and at first sight have little to do with his personal
problem. The characters in the episodes are very different from
Quidam, for they are drawn from biblical, ancient or purely fictitious
sources, and are described in an often solemn, grandiloquent style
that is apt to sound like a *pastiche* of the original sources and is far
removed from the subjective introspection of the tormented diarist.

'The Quiet Despair' (pp. 191–2) describes the relationship of a
father and son who, in spite of their apparent cordiality and cheer-
fulness, are oppressed by a common melancholy; after the father's
death the son is dominated by his memory, uncertain of the real
basis of their relationship. In 'A Leper's Soliloquy' (pp. 220 2),
Simon the Leper, though disgusted and isolated by his disease,
refuses to follow the example of his companion Manesseh who has
discovered an ointment which can turn it inwards and so conceal it
from the world. 'Solomon's Dream' (pp. 236–7) tells how Solomon
discovers that his father David, whom he has always revered, is
marked by a 'private guilt' which not only makes him an 'ungodly
man' but also creates a rift in the nature of Solomon himself who
can no longer accept his wisdom as a part of his real self. 'A Possibility' is the story of an eccentric old book-keeper whose persistent
but benevolent interest in children is explained as the result of a
moral lapse; having succumbed during a moment of intoxication to
the temptation of going with a prostitute, he is ever afterwards
tormented by the thought of having produced a child; this explains
his habit of scrutinizing each child he meets to see whether it may be
his own. 'Periander (A lesson to be inwardly digested)' (pp. 298–
308) describes how the tyrant of Corinth was cursed by the gods for
the secret sin of his wife's murder; he was treated as an enemy by
his younger son whom he wanted to be his successor. The final
episode, 'Nebuchadnezzar' (pp. 330–3) describes the king's recol-
lections of his life 'when he was a beast and ate grass' and again
portrays a man whose outward appearance differs from his inner
being.

These six episodes have been variously interpreted, but they
clearly express in symbolical form the principal obstacle standing in
the way of Quidam – Kierkegaard's efforts to find fulfilment in
marriage: his relationship with his father and their sharing of a
guilty secret. Whereas some of the episodes involve both father and
son, others portray them separately. Yet the theme of the father's
guilt and of the son's knowledge of and vicarious participation in it
seems to constitute the subject-matter of all the episodes, whether it
appears explicitly or not. When the two characters are described
together, the father is usually given the dominant role, with the son
acting as witness or confidant, but suffering intensely from the
knowledge thus acquired. We have already seen how, at the time of

the 'great earthquake', Kierkegaard was for a time demoralized by the sudden and perhaps involuntary discovery that the father whom he had so constantly and sincerely admired for his stern puritanical principles, had been guilty of a grave moral lapse.

In spite of Kierkegaard's determination never to reveal his secret,[3] many efforts have been made to uncover it. It has even been suggested that the idea of a specific cause of guilt is without foundation, and that Kierkegaard was the victim of a more general and abnormal psychological condition which had deep psychological roots (including his early relationship with his father) but no factual basis in any precise events. Various psychiatric explanations of Kierkegaard's melancholy have been put forward; he has been described as suffering from manic-depressive psychosis, schizophrenia, paranoia, masochism and the like.[4] However, instead of trying to summarize these various explanations, it may be more useful to indicate certain aspects of Kierkegaard's psychology and biography which helped to determine his own attitude towards his problem. At the same time, it is only fair to point out that some critics reject any psychological explanation of Kierkegaard's secret in favour of a specific physical cause. In a well-known essay, *Kierkegaard the Cripple*, Theodore Haecker has tried to show that Kierkegaard's troubles stemmed from his being a hunchback. That Kierkegaard was of a frail and perhaps in some ways deformed physique – in his childhood he fell and injured his back – may readily be admitted, but it seems unlikely that he would have attached such morbid feelings to a defect for which he was not responsible and which, in any case, would not have been an insuperable obstacle to marriage. If his only defect was to have been a hunchback, why could he not have revealed this 'secret' to Regine and let her decide for herself whether she still wanted him?

Kierkegaard's own observations on the subject of his secret suggest that it involved more than a merely general state of melancholy and yet less than a precise physical deformity. Moreover, it was clearly inseparable from his relations with his father and the knowledge that they shared a common shameful secret. The biographical events already described suggest two interconnected factors – first, that Kierkegaard believed that he had inherited from his father a melancholy that was connected with some form of inescapable hereditary guilt, and secondly, that this guilt was given a more precise basis by his sudden discovery of a hitherto unknown aspect of his father's life and character. At the same time, this second factor may have had an inhibiting effect upon psychological impulses which until then had not been directly associated with his father. The result, in any case, seems to have been a sense of solidarity in guilt and melancholy. This is brought out quite clearly in 'A Quiet Despair', where the father observes to his son: 'Poor child, thou art going into a quiet despair'. After his father's death, the son reflects upon these words without understanding their real meaning and without really knowing whether his father himself had truly understood them even though he 'believed that he was to blame for his son's melancholy, and the son believed he was the occasion of the father's sorrow' (p. 192).

It has been suggested that the father's melancholy was due to his life-long memory of the occasion when, as a child, he cursed God upon the Jutland heath. Yet, whatever the father's reaction to this strange incident, it seems unlikely that Kierkegaard himself would have attached so much importance to it or would have treated it as a valid reason for renouncing all idea of marriage. On the other hand, if his melancholy did not have a precise cause (whether rational or not), it is difficult to explain such a persistent feeling of guilt. Moreover, his frequent references to his secret suggest something fairly specific. The 'great earthquake' provoked by the sudden discovery of his father's weakness suggests that it originated in something far more immediate and relevant than the memory of a childhood curse. It must have been of momentous significance if it helped to make Kierkegaard feel incapable or unworthy of marriage.

Although the whole notion of 'morbid reserve' and the obsession with a presumably shameful secret suggest a direct link with sex, some more precise explanation seems to be required. This, in turn, involves reference to another factor frequently mentioned by Kierkegaard – that he was afflicted by 'a thorn in the flesh'. This expression suggests some kind of psycho-physical defect rather than a precise incident. Perhaps this notion of the 'thorn in the flesh' was linked up with an observation made in the *Journals* of 1846:

> I am in the profoundest sense an unhappy individuality which from its earliest years has been nailed fast to some suffering or other, bordering on madness, and which must have its deeper roots in a disproportion between soul and body; for (and that is what is extraordinary) it had no relation to my mind.[5]

This idea had already appeared in a curious *esquisse* for a story noted down in the *Journals* of 1843: although it does not refer explicitly to Kierkegaard himself, it may well have been inspired by reflection on his own condition:

> A genius endowed with every possible gift, capable of mastering life in all its forms and of making men obey him, discovers in his consciousness one obdurate little point of madness. He is so embittered by it that he decides to kill himself; for that one little point means everything to him, it makes him into a servile spirit, a man. Nor is it something purely exterior (for example, lameness, deafness, ugliness, etc. such things would not bother him) but touches the mind, and one would therefore imagine that the problem could be resolved with freedom; that is why it excites him.[6]

In the continuation of the 1846 entry quoted earlier, Kierkegaard mentions that he consulted a doctor 'as to whether the discord between the psychical and the physical could be resolved, so that I might realize the universal' [marriage].

> I asked him whether he thought that acting through my will, my mind was capable of reforming and transforming that funda-

mental disproportion; he would not even advise me to set my whole will-power in motion, of which he had some idea, lest I should burst everything asunder.

Consequently, Kierkegaard looked upon 'that sad discord with its attendant suffering' as 'his thorn in the flesh, his limit and his Cross'. In 1847, he again admits to having asked himself whether 'I should not collect my thoughts in order to remove, if possible, the thorn from the flesh', but he doubted whether he had 'the right to do so'.[7]

This last phrase seems significant when taken in conjunction with a more specific mention in the following year of 'being haunted by the dread of sin'; the 'thorn in the flesh' is connected with the idea of a man who 'sins against his will' and is pursued by 'sinful thoughts' which 'he would more than willingly escape and does everything to avoid'. Again in 1853, he confessed:

From an early age I have suffered from a thorn in the flesh to which the consciousness of sin and guilt has attached itself; I have felt myself to be different. This difference, this suffering, I have understood as my relation to God.[8]

According to his friend, Emil Boesen, Kierkegaard on his death-bed made a final pathetic reference to the subject. 'Like Paul', he is alleged to have said, 'I had my "thorn in the flesh"; so that I was unable to enter into the usual relations in life and thereby concluded that my task was extraordinary; and I tried to carry it out as best I could. . . . That was also what stood in the way of my marriage with Regine. I did think that it could be changed, but it could not be, so I broke off my engagement'.[9]

In view of the emphasis on the sense of guilt, and of the earliest references to the split in his personality between psychic and physical functions, it is tempting to interpret this phenomenon as some kind of sexual anomaly, perhaps a partial or complete impotence which would have cut him off from the 'universal' of marriage. Attempts to overcome this incapacity through an effort of will may have led to a deliberate provocation of sexual desire, an experience which Kierkegaard, with his strict upbringing, would naturally have considered to be sinful and which, in any case, would not have achieved its purpose.

Yet when taken by itself, this suggestion of sexual impotence or inhibition, does not explain one very important aspect of the secret, namely its indissoluble link with the father's sense of guilt. How is Kierkegaard's feeling of sexual impotence (which seems to have originated 'in an early age') to be related to his attitude towards his father's lapses from purity? In a cogently argued essay, a Danish critic, Dr. Carl Saggau,[10] has proposed an answer to this question and has based it on his examination of some of the episodes in the *Stages on Life's Way*. It has been customary, since the researches of P. A. Heiberg into Kierkegaard's youth,[11] to identify the figure of the old book-keeper in 'A Possibility' with Kierkegaard himself. Heiberg, as we have already seen, has produced some fairly convincing evidence to show that Kierkegaard himself may well have been guilty of a sexual fall in May 1836 when, in a moment of intoxication, he was perhaps taken to a brothel. This does not necessarily conflict with the previously mentioned idea of sexual impotence, for Kierkegaard's veiled references to the incident (if they are accepted as such) suggest that he had only a confused memory of what happened. Walter Lowrie follows Heiberg in his suggestion of a sexual fall but treats with sensible scepticism the idea that Kierkegaard was ever seriously worried about the consequences indicated in the story – that he had unwittingly fathered a child – and dismisses this as a merely fictitious embellishment aimed at enhancing the literary effect. It is very likely that a man who had been to a brothel would fear the possibility of venereal infection rather than paternity. Dr. Saggau, however, while making this point, suggests that the figure of the old book-keeper should be identified with Michael rather than Søren Kierkegaard. This proposal has the merit of making even the literary embellishment a part of Kierkegaard's 'confession', for it would link it up with the elder Kierkegaard's conviction that his 'great age was not a divine blessing but a curse' and that 'there must be a guilt upon the whole family, the punishment of God must be upon it; it was to disappear, wiped out by the powerful hand of God, obliterated like an unsuccessful attempt'.[12] The last part of 'A Possibility' therefore, would not be Søren Kierkegaard anxiously wondering whether he had produced a child, but his father searching his children's faces for signs of the dreaded disease. Already in 'A Quiet Despair' there is a picture of the father 'standing before his son with a sorrowful countenance and looking steadily at him' as he sees him going into a 'quiet despair' – perhaps an allusion to the same idea.

Dr. Saggau sees a further confirmation of his theory of the father's possible venereal infection in 'A Leper's Soliloquy'. When Simon the Leper found out that his companion Manesseh had obtained an 'ointment' which caused leprosy to turn inwards, he also discovered that the 'sickness did not cease'; even though the leper was henceforth able to conceal his affliction from the outside world, 'his breath could infect another and make him visibly leprous'. Simon himself refused to use the ointment, voluntarily submitting to his fate and 'freely accepting what necessity imposed'. It has been suggested that the leprosy symbolizes Kierkegaard's 'melancholy' and the ointment his ability to conceal it, but, as Dr. Saggau suggests, the story could also be taken to mean that Michael Kierkegaard sought treatment for his disease, that the symptoms actually disappeared so that even a doctor (the 'priest' of the episode) declared him cured, but that he continued to be tormented by the fear of not being completely free from the malady. Uppermost in the mind of a man who had gone on to marry and produce seven children, most of whom died young, might well have been the thought that he had passed on his disease to the members of the family, and was thus responsible for their premature deaths. In the original draft of 'A Leper's Soliloquy', we are told that one of the two lepers 'had brothers and only afterwards discovers that the same was the case with them: the whole family had fallen a victim to leprosy'.[13] Even the curious incident in the story of 'Periander' (another symbolic account of Kierkegaard's family situation) in which Periander (Michael Kierkegaard) is described as having killed his wife 'with a kick' may betray the thought that his sin was in some way responsible for his wife's death.[14]

If Søren was the son to whom the father one day unwittingly revealed his secret, he might well have come to believe that he had indeed inherited the family taint, even finding confirmation of this idea in his own sexual anomaly or 'thorn in the flesh' which he would thus tend to connect with the sense of sin and guilt. This belief would explain, for example, his reference to 'an old man who put the whole weight of his melancholy upon a child, *not to speak of something even more frightful*'.[15] Needless to say, this supposition of a hereditary taint could have been without adequate foundation, for there is no surviving medical evidence to suggest that Kierkegaard or even his father suffered from any infection of this kind, but the mere belief in such a possibility would be enough to explain its enormous importance for both men. It would certainly account for Søren's refusal to marry Regine. How could he confide to her a secret of this kind, one that concerned not only himself but also his father and the whole family? The same reason might also explain his refusal to become a priest, an idea he entertained with some persistence and anxiety in 1845. Several times he noted down the statement: *De occultis non judicat ecclesia*, which on one occasion was followed by the anxious question: 'Dare I conceal the guilt? And yet dare I reveal it myself?'[16] Although such an explanation, if valid, may help to throw light on one significant aspect of Kierkegaard's melancholy, this still remains a complex psychological or psychosomatic phenomenon. That other members of his family suffered from the same complaint is proved not only by his father's behaviour but also by his brother Peter's action in resigning his bishopric because of 'a melancholy sense of his own unworthiness'.[17]

Kierkegaard himself treated his 'melancholy' in an ambivalent way. Although he considered it to be a source of torment and unhappiness – he was the victim of 'a melancholy and its attendant suffering from which he was never entirely free even for a day',[18] he also called it his 'ultimate confidential friend' and 'the most faithful mistress he had known';[19] yet it was also a heavy burden that threatened to crush him beneath its dead weight. Indeed, Kierkegaard's own word *Tungsind* (of which 'melancholy' is perhaps not a very precise translation) already suggests the idea of a 'heavy mind'. To be 'under the sway of a prodigious melancholy' was to be subjected to an inner torpor and heaviness that paralysed the will, and yet still exposed its victim to restlessness and anxiety. T. H. Croxall has already pointed out that *Tungsind* is a very common word, often used to describe the character of Jutlanders. 'It means brooding rumination, ceaseless introspection, perpetual cogitation, lack of decision and restlessness, rather than just "listlessness".'[20] Nevertheless, this brooding melancholy is not without a certain fascination and if Kierkegaard bitterly complains of the burden it imposes on him, he also admits that he 'loves' his melancholy; he refers to 'the melancholy hatred of myself which in a melancholy man can be

almost a pleasure'.[21] This was partly because melancholy did not
exist as a merely isolated phenomenon, but involved various aspects
of his personality. The very nature of melancholy obviously linked
it up with the ceaseless activity of reflection; Kierkegaard said of
himself that with his melancholy God had given him 'an intellectual
power which had found no equal among his contemporaries'.[22] At
certain times he would try to control the influence of the mood by
the sheer power of thought and, even in moments of despair, 'I
grasped at nought but the intellectual side of man and clung fast to
it, so that the thought of my own considerable intellectual powers of
mind was my only consolation, ideas my one joy, and mankind
indifferent to me'.[23] In the *Stages* Frater Taciturnus puts forward
Quidam's reflective and intellectual nature as one of the reasons for
his inability to marry the girl he loves: 'He is essentially a thinker:
she is anything but that' (p. 390). He is, moreover, 'essentially a self-
thinker, and that in the sense of always having to have the idea on
his side in order to exist' (p. 391). But the consciousness of the
'idea' inevitably leads him to ponder the question of values, and
to feel the need to relate his existence to principles which take him
beyond the merely 'aesthetic' sphere in which the girl lives. Yet
the very impulse which makes him aware of ethical issues also
makes him realize that he is 'agonisingly prevented from realizing
perfection because he is unhappily shut off from the universally
human'.[24]

To the activity of reflection is added that of the imagination;
Quidam is not only a thinker, but also a poet, and in this respect he
again resembles the 'young man' of *Repetition*. The poetic nature
combines passion and enthusiasm with a desire for the ideal. Yet
passion, though inseparable from idealism, is by itself not enough
to resolve the problem of melancholy; with its pathos and passion,
the poetic imagination can impel the individual in the direction of
idealism, but it does not let him rest at this point; the poetic mood
has to become aware of a 'higher passion', which creates a tension
in the personality, because it does not spring from the poetic impulse
itself. When reflection is joined to imagination, it makes the individual more conscious of the ambiguity of his position and of the
conflict which exists in the heart of passion itself. Unlike poetic
passion which has opposition from outside, this higher passion is in
contradiction with itself. The individual feels the pressure of an
ideal which can no longer be satisfied at the poetic level but demands
a movement to a higher stage of existence.

Because melancholy involves this peculiar combination of
reflection and imagination, of intellect and poetry, it contains a
strongly 'dialectical' element. (The term 'dialectical' is frequently
used by Kierkegaard and with various meanings – and it appears at
a crucial point in Quidam's diary – but it usually seems to imply the
power to grasp the contradictory implications of any particular
phenomenon, to see both its negative and positive aspects.)[25] This
dialectic comes initially from the movement of passion, which
encounters an obstacle within itself, an obstacle with which it cannot
deal effectively because it exists in the realm of immediacy. If
Kierkegaard thought of himself as a poet, it was as a poet 'of a

quite peculiar kind', for 'dialectic is the essential qualification of my nature and normally dialectic is foreign to poets'.[26]

As far as Quidam is concerned, dialectic certainly involves the co-existence of contradictory impulses (the poetic and the religious) which impel him beyond his immediate situation towards a higher mode of existence. The dialectical consciousness is inseparable from the awareness of the infinite. As Frater Taciturnus puts it, he has told 'a story of unhappy love where love is dialectic in itself and in the crisis of the infinite reflection acquires a religious aspect' (p. 377). Without his melancholy reflection and imagination, Quidam would never have penetrated to the religious sphere or even envisaged its possibility. His reflection made him aware of the insufficiency of immediate feelings and, at the same time, of the power of an ethical life-view which, because it involved a collision between his own exceptional nature and the demands of the 'universal', made him 'sink back into himself' (p. 394). It was because of his 'close reserve' that he came to feel a need to transcend the aesthetic sphere and at the same time, an inability to identify himself with the universal.

Through his melancholy Quidam is thus compelled to face the religious implications of his position as an exceptional being. His dialectical nature, moreover, takes him beyond the attitude of irony which still ties existence to the 'aesthetic' sphere while making it aware of its inner tension. At first the man of morbid reserve finds a certain perverse pleasure in masking his real feelings under a cloak of irony which makes them seem the exact opposite of what they are. Yet Quidam's suffering makes it impossible for him to remain in such a detached attitude; his poetic nature is in collision with a much higher possibility than irony, for he is aware of a strong religious need: his problem is precisely one of possible guilt or madness, not of mere ironic mockery: he is beyond tragedy and comedy. In this respect Socrates already 'exemplifies a duality which poetry cannot express', but religious ideality goes beyond the Socratic viewpoint. In any case, Quidam is on the threshold of religious values, of an existence which involves guilt, repentance and the mystery of the 'forgiveness of sins'. Yet like the young man of *Repetition*, it is his creator Frater Taciturnus rather than he himself who is aware of the true situation; Quidam as yet knows only the 'demonic' in the 'direction of the religious'; he has not yet made the decisive leap into religious faith.

Kierkegaard has shocked many readers not only by describing his own personal situation in 'Guilty? Not Guilty?' (he even included the letter he wrote to Regine when he broke off the engagement) but also by presenting Regine herself in a very unfavourable light. In letting Quidam reject the girl as being spiritually unworthy of him and quite incapable of understanding his religious needs, Kierkegaard seems to be making Regine responsible for his own psychological inadequacy. In this work he was obviously trying to alleviate his own inner tensions and contradictions and 'to rid himself of all the black thoughts and dark passions within him';[27] but he was also striving, by means of his unhappy love-affair, to attain a higher stage of existence and thus give his own particular situation a much wider meaning. The study of the 'exception' was intended to bring out the essential features of every individual existence seeking genuine spiritual fulfilment. As Quidam's case makes clear, the leap into faith is never easy and although others will not be faced with his specific dilemma, they cannot be completely exempt from the suffering which accompanies the striving for religious faith.

6 Dread

An analysis of Kierkegaard's melancholy leads on to a consideration of one of the best known aspects of his philosophy – the idea of 'dread' (*Angst*).[1] Here again, we encounter an idea which had deep personal meaning for Kierkegaard and yet was given wider significance as it became linked up with a comprehensive view of human existence; although the 'melancholy' individual is particularly sensitive to the effect of dread, Kierkegaard believed that it was an experience familiar to every spiritually developed person. Because existence has constantly to be seen in the light of its possibilities, man is always 'ahead' of himself, ever moving forward to new modes of being; he comes to experience 'dread' as he is made aware of the essentially unpredictable nature of the possibilities opened up to him through the exercise of his freedom.

With the publication of *The Concept of Dread* on 17 June 1844, (and with that of the *Philosophical Fragments* four days earlier), the form of Kierkegaard's authorship underwent a significant change, for he began to abandon the imaginative portrayal of particular characters and moods for a more direct and didactic presentation of his ideas. Admittedly, *The Concept of Dread* is attributed, like the other books, to a pseudonym (Vigilius Haufniensis, the 'Watchman of Copenhagen'), but his role is unimportant as far as the contents are concerned, even though, in Kierkegaard's opinion, his presence is discernible in the work 'like a watermark'.[2] *The Concept of Dread* differs from the earlier works where the pseudonyms give the impression of being actively involved in the subject-matter and of playing the part of individuals who help to determine the perspective in which the work is to be viewed; they represent a specific existential attitude which is in harmony or conflict with that of the other characters. *The Concept of Dread*, on the other hand, abandons any appeal to the imagination or poetic feeling for a terse, austere, almost academic mode of presentation which often makes severe demands on the reader's intelligence and patience.

One of the most poetic moments of the work is to be found in Kierkegaard's dedication to his dead friend, Poul Martin Møller, who, as has already been pointed out, had a decisive influence on his early life and work. (It is worth mentioning that Kierkegaard's special esteem and affection for Møller is proved by the fact that this is the only work dedicated to a friend, all the rest being to 'the unnamed one who one day shall be named' [Regine], his father, or 'the individual, my reader'.) The original dedication of *The Concept of Dread* was more elaborate and lyrical than the published one, for it described Møller as 'my youth's enthusiasm, the mighty trumpet of my awakening, my sentiment's desired object, the confidant of my beginning, my departed friend'.[3] If the 'trumpet' sounds a dramatic note, it is not out of place in the discussion of a notion – 'dread' – which characterizes a consciousness awakened to its anguishing possibilities. The emergence of hitherto unsuspected possibilities in a person capable of both good and evil may be a disturbing, even frightening experience.

Kierkegaard was certainly aware of the influence of dread upon the development of his own life. In an important entry in the *Journals* (17 May 1843), which analyses his relationship with Regine, he calls attention to the influence of dread upon his own existence.

> But if I had had to explain myself, I should have had to initiate her into terrible things, my relation with my father, his melancholy, the eternal darkness that broods deep within, my going astray, pleasures and excesses which in the eyes of God are not perhaps so terrible, for *it was dread which drove me to excess*, and where was I to look for something to hold on to when I knew, or suspected that the one man I revered for his strength and power had wavered?[4]

In a more general way, Kierkegaard often associates his melancholy with the experience of dread: he describes himself as 'a poor man who from childhood had fallen into the most wretched melancholy, *an object of dread to himself*', and whose life had been 'embittered by the dark spot which ruins all'.[5] It was this melancholy which 'threw me for a time into sin and debauchery and yet (humanly speaking) almost more insane than guilty'. Dread and melancholy are apt to make the individual lose his grip on reality, and feel a sense of inner confusion and uncertainty which may drive him into a life of wild excess. At first unaware of the deeper significance of the experience, he fails to realize that he is being confronted by a new possibility which will enable him to move forward to a higher plane of existence. His initial reaction is to retreat into himself and shun the decisive choice which will change the entire course of his life. Quidam, the author of the diary in 'Guilty? Not-Guilty?', is no doubt recounting Kierkegaard's own experience when he writes:

> My melancholy searches everywhere for the dreadful. Then it grips me with its terror. I cannot and will not flee from it, I must endure the thought; then I find a religious composure, and only then am I free and happy, as spirit. Although I have the most enthusiastic apprehension of God's love, I have also an apprehension that He is not a dear old grandpa who sits in heaven and indulges people, but that in time and in temporal existence one must be prepared to suffer everything. . . . But he who wills in a religious sense must have a receptive attitude towards the terrible, he must open himself to it, and he has only to take care that it does not stop halfway, but that it leads him into the security of the infinite.[6]

Yet the religious significance of dread may not be apparent to the man who is absorbed in the aesthetic life. Although in *Either/Or* Kierkegaard already calls attention to the importance of dread for the 'aesthetic individual', he also points out that it is far from being typical of every form of the aesthetic life; it is experienced only by people who have attained such an exceptional intensity of feeling that they begin to experience a hitherto unacknowledged tension, the stirring of an impulse which is at variance with the demands of their immediate existence, but which they seek to overcome by plunging further into their 'aesthetic' existence. Such is the case with two characters analysed in some detail in *Either/Or* – Don Juan and Nero. The former is remarkable for the tremendous force of his desire – and indeed, it is this force which has helped to make him a legendary figure. Yet in the operatic personage sudden intimations of the darker side of his nature are discernible: in spite of the 'intensity of his passion', 'there is apprehension in that first flash, it is as if it were born in anxiety in the deep darkness – such is Don Juan's life. There is dread in him, but this dread is his energy. It is not a subjectively reflected dread, it is substantial dread. . . . Don Juan's life is not despair; but it is the whole power of sensuality, which is born in dread, and Don Juan himself is this dread, but this dread is precisely the demoniac joy of life.'[7] With Nero, on the other hand, we encounter a man who has become so satiated with pleasure that it has made him melancholy. He can be no longer satisfied with the spontaneity of immediate pleasure, and, in this sense, his experience has 'matured his soul'. Yet he is 'still a child of youth', for he will not admit the true nature of his dilemma – that he is ready for spiritual experience. Since 'the immediacy of the spirit is unable to break through', he seeks relief in increasingly refined and cruel pleasures, which serve only to disappoint and frustrate him. 'Then the spirit within him gathers like a dark cloud, its wrath broods over his soul, and it becomes an anguishing dread which ceases not even in the moment of pleasure' (II, 190). He terrifies all around him and 'the whole world trembles before his glance'. 'Yet his inmost nature is anguished dread', and he may be terrified by a child who looks at him 'in an unaccustomed way or by any casual glance'. Nero is indeed enigmatic to himself; he is like a man possessed, in spite of his limitless power and influence. His delight in terrifying others is merely an expression of his own inner dread. At the same time, such perverse individuals are capable of a 'certain good humour, finding unexpected satisfaction in some childish thing'. In the main, however, a man like Nero is the victim of melancholy, because melancholy is basically 'a hysteria of the spirit'. It is the personality striving and yet refusing to be conscious of itself 'in its eternal validity'. When this movement towards spiritual fulfilment is checked, the individual is thrust back into himself and overwhelmed by melancholy. There is, however, 'something inexplicable in melancholy', for whatever the expedients employed to relieve its pressure, it remains a mysterious element of the personality, something to which the individual clings in spite of himself. No doubt it may not be 'a bad sign', 'for as a rule only the most gifted natures are subject to it', but it none the less constitutes a sinful refusal to face the spiritual possibilities of human existence.

Whatever its particular form, therefore, dread remains a spiritual phenomenon, or rather an experience indicating the need for spiritual fulfilment. In his *Journals* Kierkegaard quotes with evident approval the statement of the German philosopher, J. G. Hamann, that 'this dread which is in the world is only the proof of our heterogeneity'.[8]

Although the sub-title of *The Concept of Dread* states that it is 'oriented in the direction of the dogmatic problem of original sin', we shall limit ourselves for the most part to the existential rather than the theological implications of this 'simple psychological deliberation'. The work clearly takes the analysis of dread in human existence much further than the brief indications of the earlier writings, where it was subordinated to a description of aesthetic and ethical attitudes. Yet the essential significance of dread had already been emphasized when it was linked up with the imminent emergence of a genuine religious awareness: the indirect manifestations of dread in the aesthetic life already show that man can never be a mere animal and that even when he seeks to limit himself to a single stage of existence, he can still feel the need for a higher mode of being. Yet it is characteristic of dread that it has no precise object. In this respect Kierkegaard distinguishes it sharply from fear which is a definite psychological reaction to a specific danger. Dread looks beyond this circumscribed area of experience, for it betokens a slumbering spiritual need. Although this impulse is not explicit, it is powerful enough to disturb the individual, to make him dissatisfied with his immediate existence. 'Spirit is dreaming in man' (p. 37). 'Dreamingly the spirit projects its own reality, but this reality is nothing' (p. 38).

Dread, therefore, is dread of 'nothing', but this 'nothing' does not signify mere negation, sheer lack of being, for, in Kierkegaard's phrase, it is 'a possibility vaguely hinted at'. This is not unexpected when we recall that the individual is anticipating a phase of existence which as yet has no precise meaning for him and lies beyond his immediate apprehension. The influence of the 'infinite' can make itself felt only negatively as a kind of lack or insufficiency in an individual who is impelled to make a new personal choice; he experiences a need to go beyond his immediate existence, but he does not understand its real purpose. At the same time, he is disturbed by the inadequacy of an existence which can no longer satisfy him; his life loses its security and stability; he has the impression of peering into an abyss – the nothingness of the infinite possibilities of his existence. 'One may liken dread to dizziness. He whose eyes chance to look down into the yawning abyss becomes dizzy' (p. 55). This dizziness is occasioned by the appearance of freedom, for in the dizziness of dread, 'freedom gazes down into its own possibility, grasping at finiteness to sustain itself'. Through his freedom man has to move to a new phase of existence, not, however, by a process of gradual transition, but by a decisive 'leap' which tears him from the security of his present existence in order to precipitate him into a new area of infinite possibility. From a psychological point of view this leap remains inexplicable, for it takes the individual into a domain of existence lying beyond the certainty of rational and scientific explanation.

A further significant aspect of the mood of dread is its ambivalence. Kierkegaard finds evidence for this at a rudimentary psychological level – for example, in the child's 'seeking after adventure', and his thirst for the prodigious, the mysterious (p. 38). In another characteristic digression he also stresses woman's ambiguous proneness to dread. Already in the 'Seducer's Diary', he had stressed the idea that woman, as the embodiment of matter, 'exists for another' (the spirit), while Quidam had rejected the girl he loved because of her lack of religious development. In the *Journals* too Kierkegaard stresses that woman, because of her greater involvement in immediacy, is particularly susceptible to dread. In *The Concept of Dread* itself he reaffirms that 'woman is more in dread than man' and sees proof of this in the contradictory emotions expressed through her 'bashfulness' (p. 60): she feels the spiritual side of her nature to be in opposition to the immediate, sensuous side, so that the 'spirit feels itself alien to the sexual'. However, at a more advanced existential level, the ambiguity of dread is obviously linked up with the experience of freedom. Since the emergence of freedom takes the individual beyond any particular finite situation to a new but undefined possibility, it both attracts and repels him. He is drawn to freedom because he is thereby fulfilling an authentic possibility of his being, but he is also made apprehensive by a 'nothingness' which seems to plunge him into an unfamiliar, indeterminate world. Dread, therefore, is 'desire for what one fears, a sympathetic antipathy'.[9]

The ambiguity of this 'sympathetic antipathy' is explained by a further characteristic: although it originates in the stirring of freedom, dread makes the individual recoil from the very freedom to which he is drawn. He is intimately involved with dread and yet feels that it also commits him to something that is outside his control and foreign to his nature. It appears as 'an alien power' which 'takes hold of the individual' (p. 39). 'Yet one cannot extricate oneself from it, does not wish to, because one is afraid, but one is attracted by what one fears'. Dread seems to paralyse the individual by its very ambiguity, making him feel that he is being 'possessed' by something stronger than himself. 'To be unfree and in the power of something else, is perhaps the greatest of all suffering for a free being'.[10] Yet this experience of unfreedom has a certain fascination, for it seems to be a necessary constituent of the experience of freedom itself.

How then does this ambivalence come about? How is it that freedom and unfreedom seem to be so interdependent? With the appearance of freedom and choice, man is faced with two different possibilities: fulfilment in accordance with his highest needs, or degradation through obedience to his lowest nature. As a free being, he becomes involved with the problem of good and evil, not in the first place as specific choices, but as fundamental possibilities of his existence: if he can become good, he can also become evil, so that the freedom of dread is inseparable from the consciousness of guilt. With the experience of dread, therefore, man abandons the state of innocence in order to face the challenge of a personal decision which affects the whole meaning of his life. The transition from innocence to guilt explains the 'dialectical' power of dread and its strange involvement with two apparently contradictory impulses:

the freedom to choose the good and at the same time the possibility of being enslaved by evil.

The problem is complicated by the apparent intrusion of 'original' sin into the experience of individual sin. Once again Kierkegaard's reflections on the subject could not ignore his own personal situation and his belief that he shared in some way his father's guilt. The connection between the two aspects of the problem becomes more obvious when we recall that the Danish word for 'original sin' (*Arvesynd*) means 'inherited sin'. More important still, Kierkegaard refuses to dismiss the problem by attributing the origin of sin to man's early history, and especially to Adam's fall; throughout his discussion he is anxious to safeguard the notion of human responsibility. Although there is a sense in which the individual is born into a sinful situation, his particular sins still remain his own responsibility; and it is with the introduction of sin into the individual consciousness that Kierkegaard is mainly concerned.

Sin appears with the loss of innocence. As soon as man feels impelled by his nature to go beyond innocence, to move from absorption in an immediate state of mind to an awareness of his 'transcendent' possibilities, he is involved in a 'mood of seriousness' which will change the entire quality of his being. This already occurs when he passes from the aesthetic to the ethical stage, for he then abandons indulgence in mere feeling for the active exercise of his will; he is no longer confronted with simple enjoyment but with the reality of a task to be achieved. In this respect, the problem involves much more than philosophical speculation. Metaphysics gives way to personal 'interest'; a general objective view of life yields to the individual's intense preoccupation with the spiritual needs of his own consciousness, and the consequent desire to satisfy them through active decision. In *Fear and Trembling*, as we have seen, Kierkegaard had also tried to show not only how the aesthetic founders upon the 'exacting ideality of the ethical', but also how the ethical itself can come into collision with the religious and take the individual towards the experience of faith 'by virtue of the absurd'. With the introduction of moral and religious values, however, the individual is confronted with guilt and sin which seem to irrupt into consciousness with a sudden leap. Moreover, this happens with every individual; it is not a phenomenon that can be located in some remote historical past. 'Every man loses innocence in the essentially same way as Adam did' (p. 33). Innocence is 'annulled' as soon as it comes into contact with something that transcends it, something 'quite different' from itself. Admittedly, the individual is both himself and the race and, from this point of view, sin may be said to have a history, but only, as Kierkegaard puts it, in the sense of having a 'continuous quantitative modification' (p. 34). It is the individual alone who is responsible for the transformation of his essential being. 'Invariably innocence is lost only by the qualitative leap of the individual'.

Perhaps it is the individual's involvement with the race which explains the common association of sin and sexuality. In so far as dread, as dread of 'nothing', reveals it to be an indefinable mood and 'a complex of sentiments which reflect themselves in themselves, coming nearer and nearer to the individual, notwithstanding that in dread they signify again essentially nothing' (p. 55), it cannot be directly related to anything as precise as sexuality. Sexuality – like other aspects of the sensuous life – is a definite characteristic which every man inherits with his entry into the world and which, in any case, merely illustrates the 'quantitative becoming of the race'; if it thereby involves sinfulness, it does so in an 'unessential' way; sexuality becomes truly sinful only when it enters the consciousness of the individual and is associated with the sin and guilt of his particular existence. Dread, therefore, still indicates the emergence of spiritual possibility and, as such, expresses far more than a particular aspect of the finite personality, but since spiritual possibility cannot remain merely empty and abstract, it has to be realized through some particular physical or psychological aspect of the personality. It is in this way that sexuality becomes involved with the possibility of sin.

From the foregoing it also emerges that dread and sin are not synonymous terms since dread is indeterminate, whilst sin is a more specific concept of theological and dogmatic significance. Dread is the psychological state preceding the appearance of sin; it 'comes as near as possible to it, and is as provocative as possible of dread, but without explaining sin, which breaks forth in the qualitative leap' (p. 82).

This leads to a final consideration – the connection between dread and time. In a sense it is the same problem as the one involving dread and sexuality; time, like sexuality, is not sinful; but its meaning is transformed as soon as it comes into contact with 'eternity'. The state of innocence is in a sense timeless, but this timeless condition is profoundly modified when man experiences a spiritual need; there emerges a new situation in which time comes to birth. Yet it cannot remain a simple concept, for the proximity of the eternal transforms the meaning of the temporal, so that the eternal and the temporal become aspects of a single synthesis which is man himself. Dread makes man aware of the possibility of the eternal; he realizes that time cannot become meaningful until it is related to the spiritual, but that, as soon as this occurs, its essential quality is changed: man is henceforth involved not in time as such, but in the 'instant'. 'No sooner is the spirit posited than the instant is there' (p. 79). The 'instant' is, properly speaking, an atom of eternity (not of time), yet an atom of eternity expressed in human existence. 'It is the finite reflection of eternity in time, its first effort to bring time to a stop' (p. 79). From this point of view the instant could not exist for paganism, which did not understand the spiritual significance of eternity. Christianity, on the other hand, interpets eternity in relation to 'the fullness of time'.

Yet in this conception of the instant, time and eternity become joined in the individual's decisive choice of his own being: dread impels the individual towards the future, but not towards a simple future determined as a mere extension of the present or past, but as a future which involves spiritual and eternal, as well as finite and temporal, possibilities. On the other hand, the spiritual notion of the future cannot be separated from other aspects of the individual's

E

existence; the concept which 'makes all things new' – 'the fullness of time' – must embrace the past as well as the future. The future does not exist as a 'thing in itself', but only as one aspect of a personal continuity which affects all aspects of man's being.

The appearance of sin does not thereby abolish dread, although it henceforth gives it a specific object. Every sin is preceded by a psychological state characterized by some degree of dread. The existence of one sin does not exclude the possibility of another, so that dread will re-emerge with the imminence of every new sin. With sin as its object, however, dread becomes dread of the evil, dread of falling more deeply into sin. At this level, therefore, dread becomes involved with remorse and repentance, which can be disarmed only by faith. Here it is not a question of examining the notion of sin as such (for this is an ethical and theological issue) but of describing 'the psychological attitudes which freedom assumes towards sin'. The purpose of dread is to lead a man to faith and to become 'a saving experience by means of faith'.

In the closing sections of the work, Kierkegaard gives his argument a characteristically personal emphasis, even though this is to some extent concealed by the philosophical and impersonal method of presentation. He goes on to describe 'dread of the good' or the 'demoniacal' – a concept that had already appeared in earlier works, especially *Fear and Trembling*, but which is now given more explicit attention. It is obviously bound up with the problem of Kierkegaard's melancholy or 'close reserve' and its relationship with his secret. At the same time, he develops a view of the demoniacal that is very modern and anticipates many later treatments of the subject.

'Dread of the good' (the 'demoniacal') starts from the feeling of isolation associated with the exceptional individual's consciousness of being different from other people: he believes himself to be cut off from the universal values governing the lives of most men. Forced back into himself, he may prove to be either a madman or a genius, but this sense of being separated from others is inescapable. In the *Journals*, Kierkegaard also insists that being 'an object of compassion tempts a man strongly to rebel against God'.[11]

The demoniacal thus starts in silence, although silence itself can be either 'the snare of the demon' or a sign of the individual's 'union with the divinity'. In either case, it takes him beyond the ethical attitude of openness and communication. Through silence, as Kierkegaard goes on to point out, the individual may be irresistibly impelled towards either good or evil: he may use his exceptional character and situation, with its attendant suffering, as a means of fulfilling the needs of his inner life and of establishing, through the activity of his freedom, an absolute relationship with God; or else, he may turn against the world, 'hating and cursing his life', setting himself above the universally human by an attitude of aggressive immorality. Whatever its particular form, the demoniacal always originates in a silent defiance of the good.

Kierkegaard is interested particularly in the 'shut-up' individual, the man of morbid reserve who deliberately immures himself in his own consciousness and makes his uniqueness and isolation an excuse for refusing to communicate with the outside world. Such a man fears, above all else, exposure to 'freedom, redemption, salvation'.

Silence, therefore, can be ambiguous, as Kierkegaard has already pointed out in his earlier works. The man of faith who tries to establish an absolute relationship with God is in large measure isolated from his fellow men; thrust back into his own inner being, he exercises his freedom in a personal way that separates him from others and makes it impossible for him to communicate with them. Even so, he sees this isolation as a challenge, as an occasion for an encounter with the eternal; his silence betokens strenuous spirituality and deep inner seriousness which are quite compatible with communication at other levels of experience. Demonic silence, on the other hand, involves a wilful refusal of revelation: it is 'shut-upness unfreely revealed'. Such an individual, by remaining defiantly immured within his own consciousness, refuses to exercise his freedom. To an active choice he prefers a complacent or perhaps anguished absorption in a particular emotional state; he steadfastly refuses to undertake the task of religious fulfilment, for he is, as it were, paralysed by the possibility of freedom. His inability or refusal to communicate with others and his rejection of ethical obligation do not stem from his devotion to some higher existential ideal, but from his continued attachment to purely human feelings: his silence is determined by his imprisonment in the finite rather than by his striving for eternity; he is thus claiming exemption from the universal before he has proved himself worthy of it.

The Concept of Dread gives various examples of this 'dread of the good', which is demoniacal by its retreat from the reality of freedom. Superstition, incredulity, are typical examples: both superstition and unbelief are forms of unfreedom, according to Kierkegaard, because the superstitious man passively submits to what he accepts as an objective power, whilst the unbeliever deliberately sets himself against the divine in a more active way. Likewise, dread of the good may be expressed through a man's inability to give true continuity to his life, as he refuses to exert his freedom and make an active choice of his existence, preferring to let his personality be fragmented into a series of aesthetic moments.

However anguishing its effects may be, this kind of dread lacks existential seriousness, because it prevents the individual from making an earnest effort to transform his existence in accordance with its true spiritual possibilities. The demoniacal person prefers to remain shut up in unhappy silence, as he refuses to move forward to a higher stage of existence – a stage which he knows to be his life's true goal but which he feels powerless to reach.

7 Existence

Although some of the main elements of Kierkegaard's thought have already been described, it has so far been a question of works which, with one exception, have presented them in an imaginative form. With *The Concept of Dread* (1844), as we have seen, Kierkegaard started to develop his ideas in a more formal, didactic manner, and this method was continued in the *Philosophical Fragments or a Fragment of Philosophy* (1844) which, though attributed to a pseudonym, Johannes Climacus, take the form of direct exposition. The most substantial and extended presentation of Kierkegaard's philosophical views was to be the *Concluding Unscientific Postscript to the Philosophical Fragments* (1846); when its bulk is compared with the short work to which it is offered as a mere comment, its title is not without irony and in spite of its serious subject-matter, it is in many respects one of the liveliest and most humorous philosophical treatises ever written. Indeed, all Kierkegaard's didactic writings contain many lyrical, personal and even whimsical passages which often give them an unexpected variety of tone and content, and reveal the close link existing between philosophical utterance and deeply felt conviction.

Fortunately for Kierkegaard the period between the publication of *The Concept of Dread* and the completion of the *Postscript* was comparatively peaceful, for it was not disturbed either by an emotional upheaval similar to the one which accompanied the breaking off of his engagement with Regine or by the violent disruption of personal life which was to take place the following year when he came into conflict with the journal *The Corsair*. For the time being he was involved in no dramatic changes. On 16 October 1844 he moved to a house in Nytorv; the following year he was to make frequent trips into the country, including a three-day sojourn at the rectory of Pedersborg, where his brother Peter was priest. After the publication of *The Stages on Life's Way* on 29 April, and *Three Discourses on Imagined Occasions* the following day (the 'occasions' were a confession, a wedding and a burial), he left for Berlin where he remained for eleven days, 13–24 May. He left no record of this trip, but presumably spent some of his time working on the manuscript of his *Postscript*.[1] One brief glimpse of his personal relations at this time is provided by a letter he sent to his niece Henriette Lund, of whom he seems to have been particularly fond.[2] He also continued to frequent the theatre; comments in the *Journals* suggest that he attended performances of Dumas's *Kean* and Bulwer Lytton's *The Lady of Lyons* which were performed in Danish translation at Copenhagen's Royal Theatre. A revival of Mozart's *Don Giovanni* between February and May 1845 attracted his attention and prompted him to write 'A passing comment on a detail in *Don Juan*'. This quiet year was remarkable especially for his crowning intellectual achievement, the composition of the *Postscript* which was eventually published on 27 February 1846.

In this work (and the *Fragments*) Kierkegaard devotes particular attention to a theme which had frequently appeared in the earlier writings but which is now subjected to a much more detailed analysis – existence. (It is to be noted that though Kierkegaard frequently uses the terms 'existence' and 'existential', he does not use 'existentialism' – a purely modern term.) The preceding chapters have already tried to show how Kierkegaard gave priority to existence over thought. In the *Philosophical Fragments* he extends this principle to all forms of existence by pointing out that a thing has to exist before it can be thought. 'I always reason from existence, not towards existence, whether I move in the sphere of palpable sensible fact or in the realm of thought'.[3] I cannot prove the existence of anything, but merely develop the conception present in my mind; existence must always be given: it is the function of reason to develop its 'ideal' implications. I cannot prove the existence of Napoleon, but only that a particular individual called Napoleon was a 'great general'. Existence as a particular fact is an absolute datum, whilst the 'essence' and 'nature' of a thing, as analysed by thought, may have only relative significance. In thus starting from the specific reality of existence rather than from a general philosophical conception, Kierkegaard was clearly challenging traditional rationalist attitudes and anticipating one of the main themes of the later 'existentialist' outlook. When this general principle is applied to human existence, it raises several problems, for man is not a static physical substance, but a being who is constantly seeking to be ahead of himself. Since this forward movement of the personality is peculiar to the human being, it is ultimately irreducible to anything other than itself; it is not susceptible to conceptual analysis, for there are no general categories by which it can be explained. Human existence cannot be made into an object of thought, because it does not express itself in the form of objective 'being' but dynamically as a process of personal 'becoming'; as such, it involves a 'passion' defying intellectual comprehension, and the most that can be done is to describe – rather than explain – its precise mode of expression. Existence, therefore, is, in the highest sense, a 'possibility', but an 'existential' possibility as opposed to the 'logical' possibility which is an abstract mental construction. In the personal sphere, to exist as possibility is not to think or to be, but to become, and the only way in which the individual can become himself is through the exercise of his freedom. An impersonal problem can have little relevance to an 'exister' who, by the sole use of his freedom, transforms the object of his concern into an occasion for making an active choice of his whole being.

If Kierkegaard speaks of the 'passion' of existence, and if he affirms that 'passion is the real thing, the real measure of man's power', and 'the age in which we live is wretched, because it is without passion', he does not mean any form of uncontrolled emotion. 'Let no one misunderstand all my talk about passion and pathos to mean that I am proclaiming any and every uncircumcised immediacy, all manner of unshaven passion'.[4] Although

Kierkegaard, as an author who is trying to bring a 'beneficial gust of feeling' into an excessively reflective age and make men aware that beyond reason lies 'enthusiasm', describes passion as an 'extraordinary power', he also insists that it must be 'purified'.[5] (In his own early life, he constantly struggled to clarify his feelings and to distinguish the true emotions at the basis of his personality from the misleading impulses which simply remained on the surface of his consciousness.) Genuine passions bear little resemblance to the unbridled emotions of the aesthetic life; they are much closer to the 'infinite personal, passionate interest'[6] of an existence that strives to realize its highest possibilities. Passion, therefore, is not to be equated with the feeling so often lauded by the Romantics – the emotional mood which 'overflows all boundaries' and abolishes clear distinctions between the various aspects of existence.

Since passion has to be related to the highest aspirations of the self, not its basest impulses, it is an essential ingredient of all valid thought; the man who incorporates genuine passion into his reflection will become a truly 'subjective thinker' by making use of 'imagination and feeling in existential inwardness, together with passion'. But he must remember that it is 'passion first and last, for it is impossible to think about existence without passion'. In other words, the thinker's passion is the very reality which he seeks to transform into an object of reflection.

Because human existence is always in movement and in a process of becoming, its decisive expression can take place only through an act which is more like a 'leap' than a gradual transition from one stage to another. Since it is not a fixed static quality, existence does not operate within the sphere of pre-established certainty, for it involves a change of quality rather than an increase in quantity. Yet the consciousness that an existential choice has absolute though unpredictable significance for the fate of the individual explains the mood of 'dread' by which it is always accompanied. The man who chooses his being in this absolute way feels that he is floating 'over seventy thousand fathoms of water'. Choice is inseparable from risk: it is an adventure into the unknown.

The meaning of this leap into the unknown is determined by the nature of the act rather than by its object; the experience of freedom is more fundamental than its particular mode of expression. In making a choice, says Kierkegaard, 'it is not so much a question of choosing the right as of the energy, the earnestness, the pathos with which one chooses'. Moreover, since freedom is an essential aspect of the human condition, it can never be expressed once and for all; as long as the individual lives, he must make new choices and strive to reach a higher stage of existence.

Kierkegaard's conception of human freedom is closely related to his view of the 'stages' or 'spheres of existence'. Since choice presupposes passing from one qualitative level to another, it is important to characterize the essential possibilities of existence. These have already been broadly indicated in the earlier works, but Kierkegaard gives a more systematic account of them in the *Postscript*, where he reaffirms that there are three 'spheres' (a word that is perhaps preferable to the 'stages') of existence: the aesthetic, the ethical and the religious, which, as we have already seen, corre-spond respectively to the attitude of the natural man concerned above all else with the enjoyment of his immediate existence; the life of the moral individual who has accepted the need to base his activity on duty and obligation and the fulfilment of the relations created by his active involvement in the 'universal human'; and the spiritual existence by which the individual is at last able to stand alone 'before God'. It is possible to pass from one sphere to the other only by means of a definite choice or leap.

In the *Postscript* Kierkegaard points out that the distinction between the three spheres is not always absolute. In the first place, the movement to the higher sphere does not abolish the lower one, but transfigures its meaning by relating it to a higher possibility; the individual who accepts the obligations of the ethical stage does not thereby repudiate the 'beauty' of the aesthetic life, but seeks to give it more stability and permanence by subordinating it to the demands of morality, so that the beautiful expresses 'eternal' value instead of the ephemeral attraction of a passing mood.[7] Secondly, there are 'boundary-zones' between the various spheres; between the aesthetic and the ethical lies irony, and between the ethical and the religious lies humour.

The ironist, as has already been stressed, is aware of an inexplicable tension or inner contradiction within himself; he knows that the aesthetic life can no longer satisfy him and that he is being impelled towards a new existential possibility. Yet he recoils from the need to make an active choice and identify himself openly with moral values, preferring to have recourse to an attitude of mocking detach-ment which obviates the necessity of taking decisive action. As opposed to this 'aesthetic' irony which merely laughs at inner con-tradictions without bringing them out into the open and resolving them, there is also a higher form of irony, ethical irony, which is a 'specific culture of the spirit'. The individual in this case may have reached the point of introducing ethical values into his inner life, but he remains absorbed in the discrepancy which he perceives to exist between himself and the outer world: 'he grasps the contradiction between the manner in which he exists inwardly and the fact that he does not outwardly express it' (p. 450). His outward life still remains in opposition to the inwardly accepted 'infinite requirement of the ethical': he protects himself against the world by assuming a kind of incognito and by refusing to let others perceive the true force of his 'ethical passion'. He thus sees that what 'interests him absolutely' does not interest others absolutely; 'this discrepancy he apprehends, and he sets the comical between himself and them, in order to be able to hold fast to the ethical in himself with still greater inward-ness' (p. 451). This means, however, that in spite of his valid apprehension of the true meaning of the ethical, he still treats it as a mere possibility, for he has failed to translate his inner conviction into personal action by existing openly in the truth which is so clearly perceived.

Between the ethical and the religious lies the domain of humour. Humour differs from irony in that it is further from the aesthetic stage, for it has achieved an explicit awareness of spiritual needs.

But the humorist deliberately projects those needs (for example, the need to give his life an absolute, eternal meaning) on to objects and aims which are incommensurate with a genuinely religious aspiration. Humour, therefore, involves a contradiction between the consciousness of a God-relationship and its practical realization in personal endeavour. The humorist has no personal relationship with God, but turns himself into a 'jesting and yet profound exchange-centre for these [religious] transactions' (p. 451). Just as the ethicist makes irony his incognito, so does the religious man conceal his true feelings beneath his humour. In each case, the higher stage of existence is envisaged as a mere possibility, not as a living part of experience. Although the ironist and the humorist achieve a higher mode of existence than the aesthetic individual in so far as they are 'inwardly committed', they seek to avoid the pain of inner contradiction by treating it as a mere possibility instead of a 'dreadful reality'.

If 'existence' thus stands opposed to thought and mere reflection, and if it shuns objective possibility as an end in itself (while still accepting the fulfilment of spiritual possibility as the only valid goal of life's endeavour), it certainly does not follow, as Kierkegaard is at pains to point out, that existence is thereby made 'thoughtless' (p. 112). The essential point is for the true thinker to realize that existence cannot be reduced to a mere object of reflection and transformed into a logical system or a rounded and tidy pattern of abstractions, because it involves a constant effort to transcend inner contradictions by *becoming* something higher instead of merely *being* what it is; existence defies any attempt to comprehend it as a single static concept. Furthermore, the very movement which is at the heart of existence shows that there is something which cannot be thought, namely, existence itself (p. 274). Whereas abstract thought constantly looks outwards, seeking to grasp some objective possibility, existence is 'a category on which pure thought must suffer shipwreck' (p. 278). This is the point at which personal becoming separates itself from the merely cognitive attitude.

> The only reality to which an existing individual may have a relation that is more than cognitive, is his own reality, the fact that he exists; this reality constitutes his absolute interest.

Kierkegaard thus rejects the Cartesian principle of the *cogito* as the starting-point for rational certainty. When personal consciousness is properly deepened, it goes beyond the 'certainty of reflection' and plunges the individual into a state of 'dread' as he is made aware of the existential possibilities thus opening up before him.

As soon as the individual becomes 'intensely interested' in the authentic possibilities of his existence, he is conscious of their ambiguity: he is confronted with two distinct and yet inseparable aspects of existence – the temporal and the eternal; as an existing individual who seeks an absolute meaning for his life, he is 'the child of the finite and the infinite'. It is on this essential point that the aesthetic and reflective attitude is in direct opposition to the religious outlook; whereas the former seeks to grasp reality by understanding it as a clear concept and by making it part of a coherent system of thought, the latter's involvement with the eternal induces the individual to abandon the domain of abstract speculation for a decisive effort to make his temporal existence an expression of infinite personal concern. That is why the true individual must pass constantly from the perception of mere possibility to the activity of earnest endeavour, for only in this way can his personality combine its finite and infinite aspects.

It is on this vital issue that Kierkegaard sees himself as an un-relenting opponent of Hegel. Kierkegaard's philosophy starts from the inescapable assumption that it is impossible to conceptualize a 'dialectical' reality like that of human existence; there is no fixed universal quality capable of embracing all types of particulars and of reducing them – through rational analysis – to a common intellectual denominator; there are only individual existents whose very nature is to repel thought. Abstract thought, in seeking to objectify existence and so remove its unique 'dialectical' character, moves away from reality. However 'interested' he may be in the eternal, the individual cannot move from his immediate situation into a domain of pure thought; he has to hold fast to eternity in the midst of finite existence itself, and it is from this very fact that all the basic characteristics of authentic human nature can ultimately be derived.

> Because abstract thought is *sub specie aeterni*, it ignores the concrete and the temporal, the existential process, the predica-ment of the existing individual arising from his being a synthesis of the temporal and the eternal situated in existence. . . . Abstract thought cannot take cognizance of this contradiction, since the very process of abstraction prevents the contradiction from arising.[8]

Kierkegaard's long and arduous campaign against Hegel concen-trates on this central issue of the meaning of individual existence.[9] He mocks at the German philosopher for thinking in grandiose terms which none the less ignore the very reality which must first and foremost affect every human being – his own reality. Striving and becoming are features of existence, because they embody the individual's attempts to bring reality into his life by combining the infinite and the finite, the eternal and the temporal. Hegel, on the other hand, while acknowledging the contradictory and dialectical features of human existence, seeks to reconcile them by reducing them to a subordinate aspect of an all-embracing Absolute which alone has ultimate meaning. But at what terrible cost! Is not Hegel in his ambitious search for the absolute forgetting his own particular existence? He is like a man who builds a magnificent palace and yet continues to live in an old shack nearby! That is why there is so much talk in Hegel of the 'world-historical' and so little of the individual person. Yet the individual is – or ought to be – concerned with a single issue which overshadows all the rest and reduces the world-historical to insignificance – his relationship with God. Once again we see the opposition between Hegelian philosophizing and individual existence; the former seeks to reduce everything to the realm of immanence by making it the expression of an ultimate 'pantheistic' Absolute, whilst the latter holds fast to the contradictions produced by the intimate relationship of the finite and the infinite.[9]

For the ethical and religious individual the principal task is to become 'subjective'. It will already be obvious that Kierkegaard does not mean by 'subjectivity' mere subjectivism, which is the self's wilful and foolish refusal to face the reality of its situation. Whereas subjectivism is a way of escaping from reality, subjectivity represents the individual's true 'inwardness', his intense effort to grasp something that has absolute significance for his life; it seeks to find and accept a truth which involves active personal appropriation. Moreover, it is this very factor of personal appropriation which gives truth its reality. Kierkegaard criticizes scientific ideas for being too impersonal and for dealing with mere approximations based on an effort to understand the meaning of the external world; existence, on the other hand, must have absolute significance for the individual personality.

> For an objective reflection the truth becomes an object. For a subjective reflection, the truth becomes a matter of appropriation, of inwardness, of subjectivity, and thought must probe more and more deeply into the subject and his subjectivity [p. 171].

In order to find a relationship to eternal truth and to seek truth with 'the passion of the infinite', a man may have to realize that the truth he passionately desires is tied to an 'objective uncertainty'. This is why personal appropriation is inseparable from the experience of dread before existential possibilities which may at first sight seem to be 'nothing'. Just as an individual choice cannot rest upon any objective guarantee of its rightness, so existential truth cannot rest upon any preconceived certainty. The individual recognizes that it is only in existential affirmation that the truth can be reached, for it is this act alone which has absolute significance for him. This does not mean that Kierkegaard is questioning the validity of certain forms of scientific knowledge when they are related to their own proper sphere of reason and experiment; he is simply asserting that, for the individual, such researches can never have absolute personal value: it still remains his responsibility to decide what science or any other 'relative' form of knowledge means to him.

What Kierkegaard is seeking to criticize through his attacks upon objective thought is the mistaken attempt to apply scientific and similar criteria to the establishment of 'existential' truth. He illustrates his point by referring to the alleged proofs for the immortality of the soul. How is it possible for the individual to examine the question of the immortality of the soul in a detached rational manner when it is inseparable from the struggle to find a meaning for his own existence? Immortality is not susceptible of valid proof, because any possible proof is constituted by 'the most passionate interest of subjectivity'. To consider the question of immortality in this way is to link it to a 'deed' – the expression of immortality in our own existence; as long as this active concern is lacking, the question can have no meaning. If, on the other hand, we seek to consider the problem objectively, the very faith which is an essential condition for its resolution will steadily diminish: as proofs become more frequent, certitude becomes weaker. Questions of existential truth depend in the last resort on the spiritual striving of the individual and so on his personal choice of himself. It is not until they are related to that basic choice that they can have meaning for him. The existential act must always precede any theoretical consideration of its content, for otherwise reflection remains merely empty and abstract.

It is this concern with the reality of existence which explains Kierkegaard's admiration for Socrates. The Master's thesis on *The Concept of Irony* had consistently called attention to the importance of Socrates' personal attitude towards the problem of knowledge; the Socratic method was not a mere intellectual device, but a means of getting closer to the reality of the human condition. Nevertheless, Kierkegaard had there criticized Socrates' conclusions for being too negative, alleging that in his eagerness to demolish other people's ideas, Socrates not only failed to put forward constructive ideas of his own, but also ignored the objectivity of social and religious values. In his later works, however, Kierkegaard withdrew this criticism, affirming that it had been made under the influence of Hegel, and he gave Socrates more positive significance as a thinker who was closely concerned with embodying ethical values in his own existence and with adopting a positive personal attitude towards the truth instead of losing himself in intellectual abstraction. 'When Socrates believed that there was a God, he held fast to the objective uncertainty with the whole passion of his inwardness' (*Postscript*, p. 188). It was 'the everlasting merit of Socratic wisdom to have become aware of the essential significance of existence, of the fact that the knower is an existing individual' (p. 183). No thinker who fails to recognize this fundamental fact can hope to make any advance on Socrates, and, according to Kierkegaard, a grave limitation of contemporary philosophy, and especially of Hegelianism, is not to have recognized the need to relate intellectual problems to the experience of inner appropriation, for only in this way can they become real. 'Socratic existential inwardness' is a lesson that must be learned by every thinker who seeks the truth.

In spite of all this, the *Philosophical Fragments* already make it clear that the Greek conception of truth was subject to a very serious limitation, and, in one vital respect, differed profoundly from the true 'existential' viewpoint. Although Socrates was aware of man's need to establish a personal relationship with the eternal, that is, with a truth which would have absolute significance for him, he believed that there was a sense in which this truth already existed in the human being and that the main problem was to bring it to birth – hence the famous method of Socratic 'midwifery': when a man comes to know himself absolutely, he will also comprehend the meaning of the eternal within him. His main task, therefore, must be to overcome the ignorance which prevents him from attaining insight into the truth; it is a question of devising a method which will enable him to obtain truth by 'recollection'. To do this, he no doubt needs a teacher, but this teacher is merely an occasion for the individual to discover something that already exists within himself; with the attainment of greater insight and rationality, the individual can overcome the limitations of his ignorance and find his own solution to his problem.

Kierkegaard's conception of the relationship between the eternal and the temporal is quite different. Because he sees existence as the meeting-point of time and eternity, he rejects the Platonic principle of 'recollection' in favour of a stress upon the idea of paradox. In this he is clearly influenced by his acceptance of the Christian doctrine of the Incarnation: God has revealed Himself at a particular historical moment, thereby creating a double difficulty for man: absolute truth seems henceforth to depend largely on his relationship with this historical event, whilst it is difficult to see how God himself can be embodied in a temporal medium. Although the specifically religious implications of this viewpoint will be discussed in connection with Kierkegaard's Christian outlook, it will be apposite to point out here that he shifts the main philosophical emphasis from ignorance to sin. This is already apparent in the importance accorded to 'dread' as an affective reaction to the possibility of sin in the individual. Ultimately it is God's entry into time which creates the main paradox of Kierkegaard's reflection upon existence; because God has revealed himself from above, it is necessary to have a Teacher who can offer more than the immanent wisdom (however great) of a Socrates who relied on the individual's capacity to become aware of what already lay buried in the depths of his own being; the Teacher has to create the conditions for the receipt of truth as well as the essence of truth itself: he has to make the individual aware that his main problem does not concern ignorance but sin.

It is this priority accorded to sin over ignorance which lends further support to Kierkegaard's decisive rejection of all forms of philosophical idealism which, by establishing the essential unity of being and thought, seek to reconcile the various differences and contradictions of human experience by the use of some higher unifying principle. Sin takes the individual beyond any abstract, monistic principle by relating him to a genuinely transcendent reality – God. It is only through an active relationship with an absolutely transcendent God, and through standing alone 'before God' who is qualitatively different from himself, that the individual can attain personal fulfilment, not simply as a being who seeks the truth through the use of his reason, but as one who also achieves salvation through the conquest of sin. Yet if God thereby becomes more 'objective' than the principle of idealism, His 'objectivity' is of a special kind, since He can enter into relationship with a finite being who is wholly other than Himself, and, by so doing, change the essential quality of his being.

It is man's overriding concern with his need to establish a personal relationship with God which makes the question of philosophical proofs of God's existence seem of very minor importance. In any case, there must be a sense in which reason can never know God, because it is a finite power limited to the domain of human experience. Since man does not have the capacity to bring the truth out of his own being, he can no longer rely upon his reason to save him from ignorance and sin. If this brings him face to face with a paradox, it does not mean that a paradox ought to be shunned, for reason itself is constantly being challenged to resolve contradictions and to push further into the meaning of things by grasping and resolving their apparently contradictory aspects.

> The paradox is the source of the thinker's passion, and the thinker without a paradox is like a lover without feeling: a paltry mediocrity. (*Phil. Frag.*)

Paradox, as Kierkegaard insists in *Journals*, is the 'pathos of intellectual life', just as passions are characteristic of great souls; the thinker alone can grasp paradoxes which are 'grandiose thoughts in embryo'.[10] Now just as it is the 'highest pitch of passion to will its own downfall', so it is the 'supreme passion of reason to seek a collision, though this collision must in one way or another prove its undoing'. Reason, therefore, is constantly seeking to go beyond the valid limits of its own activity, to grasp what it cannot as yet comprehend. 'The supreme paradox of all thought is the attempt to discover something that thought cannot think.'

In one way this difficulty is characteristic of all intellectual reflection in so far as it is directed on something outside itself; there is a point beyond which understanding cannot go, even in regard to the familiar world. This limitation becomes particularly important as soon as we encounter a transcendent reality, an Unknown completely different from ourselves, for we are now dealing with a special kind of paradox. Our initial difficulty is to lay hold of the existence of an absolute unlikeness which defies all rational comprehension. In any case, reason is unable to conceive unlikeness except in terms of itself; it always tends to think of unlikeness as the opposite of itself (irrational, absurd, monstrous, etc.); in seeking to grasp the unknown, it merely 'confounds the like and the unlike'. When reason encounters a God that is absolutely unlike man and when this unlikeness involves not merely ignorance but sin, it is presented with an absolute paradox that cannot be overcome by the individual's own rational efforts. Only God can create the conditions capable of freeing him from his bondage to untruth. Since the effect of reason is in fact to know the paradox only as something which it cannot conceive, the paradox must be grasped in another way, and this is the precise function of faith. God's transcendence has to be approached by faith rather than by reason, for faith alone is capable of the 'passion' necessary for resolving the difficulty inherent in this supreme paradox.

Because man may come into relationship with God only by an 'absurd' personal response which goes beyond reason, he is once again made aware of his freedom. It is his freedom which makes possible his active response to God's revelation of himself in time. God, as it were, takes the initiative by breaking into history and presenting

himself to man in a personal encounter. But man still has the responsibility of deciding what this encounter means to him: since he is free
he may be repelled or offended by the Absolute Paradox of God's
disclosure of himself in human temporal form: he may turn away
from the Paradox or he may choose to stand 'alone before God'.
Whereas the rational attitude merely seeks to comprehend God's
nature, faith tries to lay hold of God's existence as an occasion for
personal choice. The paradox, therefore, is a unique feature of
spiritual existence – a truth which, according to Kierkegaard, Kant
did not perceive; he failed to see that 'the inexplicable, the paradox,
is a category of its own'.[11]

The conception of existence as paradox constantly leads us back
to the personal reality of the individual. So important is this point
that Kierkegaard considered the individual (*den Enkelte*) to be the
special being to whom his work was addressed and dedicated – 'the
individual whom with joy and gratitude I call my reader'. The
individual was his 'category'. 'If I were to desire an inscription for
my tombstone, I should desire none other than "That Individual" –
if that is not now understood, it surely will be'.[12] The individual, he
affirmed, was the 'most decisive thing', the 'category through which,
in a religious respect, this age, all history, the human race as a whole,
must pass'.

Existence and the personal reality of the individual are to a large
extent synonymous, because they not only defy conceptual definition
in philosophical terms, but are also incompatible with the 'untruth'
of the 'abstract, fantastical, impersonal crowd – the public which
excludes God as the middle term' and weakens the sense of personal
responsibility by reducing it to 'a mere fraction'.[13]

> In his conscience, and in his responsibility before God, i.e.
> through his consciousness of being eternal, everyone is an
> individual. A mass he never becomes, nor lost in a 'public'. . . .
> His responsibility towards eternity saves him from that which
> characterizes the animals, namely that they are a crowd, a mass,
> a public, or whatever other impulse it is which causes one to have
> to speak of human beings as if one were speaking of a drove of
> oxen.[14]

Religious truth is opposed to the anonymity of the crowd, for 'the
individual' is the category of 'spiritual awakening'.

Nevertheless, the 'inwardness' and 'subjectivity' of individual
existence, though inseparable from the paradoxical nature of man as
a synthesis of the temporal and the eternal, are not intended to make
him an isolated being, who is merely different from others. The
individual does not exist in empty solitude; he is 'alone before God'.
It is his task to turn to 'God, personally as a single person, quite
literally as a single person'. If to be an individual is to admit the
need for a relationship with an absolutely transcendent being, God,
this relationship cannot be understood in rational terms, for it is a
fundamentally personal one. God Himself is the supreme Person
and man has to become a true person in order to enter into relationship with Him. 'In this purely personal relation between God as

personal being and the believer as personal being, in *existence*, is to be found the concept of faith.'[15] Because the religious individual is striving to express in his existence a spiritual reality which every other man is also called upon to express in *his* being, the notion of personal existence, when properly understood, will be seen to possess universal as well as individual significance, the essential point being that the 'universal' cannot be expressed in abstract terms but only through the 'true inwardness' of living faith.

8 Inner Development (1846-50)

In 1846 Kierkegaard completed the exposition of his main philo-sophical ideas with the publication of the *Concluding Unscientific Postscript* which he seems to have intended to be his last major work. We shall see that the rest of his authorship was to a large extent occasioned by the events of his personal life and inspired by a precise religious purpose which had been merely implicit in the earlier writings. Although the *Edifying Discourses* accompanying the secular works had constantly testified to Kierkegaard's pre-occupation with Christianity, the Christian theme had, as it were, only run parallel to the analysis of human existence. Henceforth, however, it was to occupy a central position in his thought. From time to time he would continue to show that he was still capable of producing an 'aesthetic' work, but these excursions into non-religious fields were rare and of only very minor significance for the understanding of his main ideas.

The *Postscript* had contained an important section entitled 'A Glance at a contemporary effort in Danish Literature';[1] in this essay, Kierkegaard paused to look back at his whole production with a view to explaining its overall purpose and the interdependence of the various parts. In particular, he was anxious to stress his role as a writer who sought to remind his age that its obsession with objective, impersonal knowledge had made it forget 'what it means to exist and what inwardness is': to exist and to know, he declared, are two different things. This concern with existential inwardness also explained the order of his books, which described the develop-ment of inwardness through its various stages and inner conflicts as it moved from the aesthetic to the religious life and from the 'enjoyment' (or perdition) of the 'natural' man to the 'suffering' of spiritual fulfilment 'before God'. In the same essay, Kierkegaard pointed out that his desire to describe inwardness in living terms was responsible for his use of pseudonyms and indirect communication. The tenor of this essay and of the personal declaration appended to the whole work suggests that Kierkegaard now saw his task as more or less complete.

For a time he thought of becoming a minister in a small country parish and of making his literary activity incidental to his new calling. Certainly he had some reason to be content with what he had so far achieved in the literary field. Although his books had puzzled and disconcerted many of his contemporaries, his reputation in Copenhagen seems to have been high. Moreover, his personal life was not without its pleasurable moments. Apart from the esteem accorded to him by the cultivated members of society, he found particular satisfaction in the conversation of ordinary citizens, and he was often to be seen with them in the streets. What he lacked in physical attraction – he had a small delicate physique, being very round-shouldered and thin-legged, with a great tuft of hair sticking up above his forehead, a wide mouth and protruding teeth – was more than offset by his charming smile, friendly manner and lively conversation. There was one curious aspect of these encounters: those who wished to talk to him had to ask him to stand still, because he had a curious side-long gait which made it difficult for anyone to walk with him without being pushed aside! As so often in this period of his life, he showed that he was far from being the 'gloomy Dane' with whom he was subsequently to be identified.

In spite of his idea of becoming a minister, Kierkegaard found it difficult to make a definite decision about his future. His long and arduous intellectual efforts had left him in a frequently tense and unsettled mood. Between 1844 and 1848, he made several changes of residence, often for apparently trivial reasons. He lived for a time in the house where he was born, which, with his brother, he had inherited from his father. He was, however, easily worried by small discomforts; on one occasion he was upset by the smell of a nearby tannery, while on another he was irked by the sunlight reflected from the windows of a house opposite his own. He also ran into financial troubles. Although his father had left a considerable fortune, and Kierkegaard could have lived without financial worries, his style of life proved very expensive.[2] His authorship cost him a lot of money: in order to preserve his anonymity, he employed secretaries to copy out his manuscripts; he also obtained very little from his books which he printed at his own expense. (The *Postscript* sold only fifty-five copies.) He spent large sums on his frequent trips to Sjaelland which sometimes lasted several days: he liked to travel in comfort and usually took with him his faithful servant, Anders Westergaard. He was prompted to spend his money by the thought that he would die young, and, as we have seen, he did not expect to pass his thirty-fourth birthday.

A turning-point in his career was his quarrel with a satirical newspaper called *The Corsair*; this event, which ought to have been of trivial importance to a man of Kierkegaard's intellect and reputation, was to change the whole pattern of his life. The psychological aspects of this affair show how the intensity of his personal feelings was in no way proportionate to the events responsible for them. *The Corsair* was run by an enterprising but not too scrupulous young Jew called Goldschmidt, who sought to combine cultural pretension with a malicious delight in relating scandalous gossip about distinguished contemporaries; in spite of its ostensible intellectual appeal, the paper exploited scandal for financial gain, and achieved a wide circulation. At first, Kierkegaard was quite well disposed towards Goldschmidt, who in his turn had a genuine admiration for Kierkegaard. Indeed, an article in the paper had praised Victor Eremita, the pseudonymous editor of *Either/Or*, for having produced an immortal work.

One of the paper's chief collaborators was a certain P. L. Møller, whom Kierkegaard had known in his student days as a lively, witty and immoral young man, with a particular interest in aesthetics, and who may have served as a model for Johannes in 'The Seducer's Diary'. Having failed to pass his university examinations, Møller had become a journalist, while still retaining hopes of following a

F

serious intellectual career. In spite of his lack of academic qualifications, he aspired to the Chair of Aesthetics, which had previously been held by the distinguished poet Oehlenschläger, and he was encouraged in his ambition by the award of a gold medal for a prize essay and the publication of a certain number of poems. In a literary review called *Gaea* he had published an article, which had not only discussed Kierkegaard's work in a hostile spirit, but had made unfavourable allusions to his character; more especially, it had called attention to the personal significance of 'Guilty? Not Guilty?' which was blamed – perhaps not without justification – for its indiscretion and bad taste. Kierkegaard was obviously not pleased to have the more intimate side of the work given public prominence in this way and when he replied to Møller's criticism in *The Fatherland*, he did him irreparable harm by revealing his connection with *The Corsair*, for Møller was immediately deprived of any chance of getting Oehlenschläger's Chair. Møller was so shattered by all this that he eventually left Denmark and died in poverty. Kierkegaard, however, was not content to leave the matter there. He did not want to be given preferential treatment by a paper that slandered respectable contemporaries and he asked *The Corsair* to treat him too as a target for its attacks. His wish was soon granted and he found himself the object of relentless and vicious satire. Nothing was spared – his physical appearance, dress and character were all held up to ridicule: the paper made fun of his thin legs; even his trousers became a subject of jest, for it was alleged that one leg was longer than the other. When he went out, people would pause to stare at him; children ran after him in the street, shouting 'Either, Or!'. In the meantime, Goldschmidt seems to have hoped for a reconciliation, and perhaps intended to speak to Kierkegaard, but when he met him in the street, was disconcerted by a 'great wild look' which Kierkegaard gave him as he passed. Goldschmidt was so 'grieved and upset' by this that he soon decided to give up *The Corsair*. For a time, he went abroad and on his return to Denmark started up a monthly magazine of a much more respectable kind.

Unfortunately Goldschmidt's action was too late to prevent *The Corsair*'s campaign from having disastrous repercussions on Kierkegaard's inner life; he was driven into himself and cut off from his previously invigorating contacts with his fellow-citizens. The *Journals* of this period give ample evidence of his acute distress. Although his rational self realized that the attacks did not deserve serious attention, his natural sensitivity made it impossible for him to ignore them. At the same time, he became increasingly uncertain about his future. Since he was henceforth determined to 'stand his ground', he felt that he could no longer seek refuge in the priesthood. He eventually decided that the only effective way of dealing with the situation was to renew his literary production. The corrupt state of society, of which he considered *The Corsair* to be but one obvious example, made him still more conscious of the importance of religious values, so that he eventually came to realize that the earlier method of 'indirect communication' was not suited to an age that required a plainer and simpler lesson. Moreover, his isolation increased his own personal need to write, as he makes clear in his *Journals* for 1847:

Only when I am producing do I feel well. Then I forget all the discomforts of life, all suffering, then I am in my thought and happy. If I let it alone even for a couple of days, I immediately get ill, overwhelmed, troubled, my head heavy and burdened. An impulse such as that, so rich, so inexhaustible, which after having held out day after day for five or six years, still flows as richly as ever, an impulse such as that must also be a call from God.[4]

As he said on another occasion, 'I need the magic of productivity in order to forget the paltry pettiness of life'.

If Kierkegaard's contemporaries seemed to be hostile towards him, King Christian VIII showed his interest by sending him several invitations in 1846 and 1847. Apparently these invitations were not accepted as often as the king would have wished. Perhaps Kierkegaard feared to become an official supporter of the established order; in spite of the conservatism of his political views, he was not anxious to be associated with any specific cause. He boldly told the king: 'I have the honour to serve a higher power, for the sake of which I have staked my life'.[5] Nevertheless, the conversations seem to have been friendly and uninhibited. It was typical of Kierkegaard's high opinion of his work that he did not hesitate to tell the king that 'it was a miserable existence to be a genius in a provincial town'.

Of more lasting significance was an event of a very different kind. A clergyman called Adler believed that he had received a special revelation from God. One day he thought he heard 'a hoarse voice' telling him to burn his writings about Hegel and to remain faithful to the Bible. This 'revelation' not unnaturally brought him into conflict with the Church and he was eventually deprived of his living. From the very first the incident intrigued Kierkegaard, who seems to have been approached by Adler as a writer capable of understanding and supporting him. Adler considered Kierkegaard to be the 'John the Baptist' who would herald his own appearance as the Messiah! Although Kierkegaard never took Adler himself seriously, he soon began to examine aspects of the case in a study entitled *The Book on Adler*. He was at first deterred from publishing this work by the personal nature of the subject-matter; while condemning Adler's views, he felt no personal animosity against him and no doubt did not wish to add to the troubles which the unfortunate clergyman had already brought upon himself by his rash claims. Kierkegaard, however, attached considerable importance to the book and thought of publishing it in 1848 as *A Cycle of Ethico-Religious Treatises*. Only one part appeared in his lifetime – 'The difference between a genius and an apostle', which was published in 1849 under the pseudonym of 'H.H.', with another short treatise. 'Has a man a right to let himself be put to death for the truth?'

These issues were of growing concern to Kierkegaard, not of course because he believed himself in danger of physical martyrdom, but because his isolated position, as well as his opposition to contemporary values, made him more and more conscious of himself as 'an exception'; he felt that he had been called, perhaps by God, to serve as the 'extraordinary'. If his work was addressed increasingly to the 'individual', he himself was more and more aware of his own exceptional position. He had no doubt about the confusion existing in the mind of the bizarre Adler, but he saw this case as an important challenge to existing values and an occasion for raising the question of what it meant to be a Christian. In spite of his errors, Adler had come 'into serious touch with what it means to become a Christian'. It was this very conviction which caused him to lose his living: 'as a heathen he became a Christian priest, and when he had got somewhat nearer to the experience of becoming a Christian, he was deposed'.

The encounter with Adler made Kierkegaard realize how firmly opposed was his own outlook to an age that was being increasingly dominated by the 'masses'. In a *Literary Review*[6] published in 1846, he had already launched a vigorous attack upon 'the present age', blaming it for preferring superficial reflection to genuine passion, and soulless mediocrity to a genuine concern for individuals. After his experiences with Adler and the events following *The Corsair*'s campaign against him, Kierkegaard came to feel that it was not only his work but his personal existence which would serve as a challenge to the false values of his time. Whatever his mistakes, Adler had rightly seen that Christianity had to have living significance and that its spirit could not be effectively expressed in fossilized institutions but only in individuals who attained an active relationship with God. In Kierkegaard's view, Adler's erroneous belief in 'revelation' did not affect the main issue: there still remained a contradiction between official 'Christendom' and living Christianity. This was the theme to which Kierkegaard devoted increasing attention in his last years, when he became engaged in a violent attack on 'Christendom'.

Meanwhile, the essay on 'The difference between a genius and an apostle' had called attention to an important issue which was prominent in all his later works. The apostle's role derived directly from his immediate relationship with Christ, so that his position did not rest upon his own personal attributes, but upon divine authority; it was Christ who had singled him out for his role. Genius, on the other hand, is quite different, for it involves a natural gift exercised by the individual in his own right. 'Divine revelation' and 'poetic inspiration' must always be opposed, and Christianity can only suffer from foolish attempts to confuse the two categories. The genius is clearly closer to man than the apostle, for he expresses powers which, though exceptional in one sense, are of human origin, whilst the apostle may, humanly speaking, seem quite unqualified for his task, but still be called by God to perform His will. In this respect, the question of the paradox, already examined, reappears in a new co text. The work of a genius may seem to constitute a paradox, but this is simply because his ideas are in advance of his time; they are paradoxical only in relation to the understanding of his contemporaries, not because of their intrinsic nature. 'Ultimately the race will assimilate what was once a paradox in such a way that it is no longer paradoxical'.[7] The paradox communicated by the apostle can never be overcome in this way, because it does not originate in a human source, but in Christ himself – in Christ who will always remain the supreme Paradox, ever beyond the grasp of human understanding. It follows, therefore, that the apostle cannot be recognized in the same way as the genius. Whereas the latter must ultimately be accepted for his own inherent qualities, the apostle's message, which derives from an authority greater than his own, can be received only with faith – a faith that comes from God and not from the human will. The only human proof of the apostle's mission is his willingness to undergo martyrdom and to die for the message for which God alone is ultimately responsible.

While Kierkegaard's writings were revealing a more and more consistent religious purpose, his personal life was still subjected to sudden oscillations of mood. At Easter, 1848, he experienced a religious conversion similar to the one which had occurred a few years earlier:

> Wednesday, 19th April, 1848. N.B. My whole being is changed. My reserve and isolation is broken – I must speak. Lord, give thy grace.... Alas, she could not break the silence of my melancholy. ... Now with God's help, I shall be myself, I believe that Christ will help me to be victorious over my melancholy, and so I shall become a priest.[8]

Yet a few days later he was forced to admit his inability to overcome his melancholy:

> N.B. 24th April, 1848, Easter Monday. No, no, my self-isolation cannot be broken, at least not now. The thought of breaking it occupied me so much, and at all times, that it only becomes more and more firmly embedded.[9]

He found some consolation in speaking of his problem to his doctor, even though it did not produce a remedy. More important still was the deep satisfaction he once again found in his intellectual activity. 'My intellectual work satisfies me so, and makes me gladly acquiesce in everything as long as I may only belong to it.'[10]

He was certainly justified in this claim, for it was at this time that he produced two of his most remarkable religious works – *The Sickness unto Death* (published in 1849, but written in the previous year) and *Training in Christianity* (which, though published in 1850, was also written in 1848). Apart from these serious didactic books, Kierkegaard showed that he was still capable of aesthetic production by publishing under the pseudonym of 'Inter et Inter' *The Crisis and a Crisis in the Life of an Actress* – to be followed, in December of the same year, by the composition of an essay (which remained unpublished) on 'Herr Phister as Scipio in the comic opera *Ludovic*'.

Attention has already been called to Kierkegaard's early enthusiasm for the theatre, and it is clear from these essays that his interest was maintained in later life. Although no particular person is mentioned in *The Crisis*, which was concerned with the problem of dramatic art rather than with any specific individual, Kierkegaard had in mind a famous actress of the time, Fru Heiberg, the young wife of Denmark's most distinguished and versatile writer, Johann Ludvig Heiberg (1791–1860). In 1847 she decided to appear once again as Shakespeare's Juliet – a role in which she had been very successful in her early years. It was this performance of *Romeo and Juliet* which prompted Kierkegaard to write his 'aesthetic' piece. Although Kierkegaard did not mention her name, Fru Heiberg rightly believed that he had her in mind – and her belief was subsequently confirmed when the author sent her a copy of his essay with a flattering dedication. In spite of his dislike of Heiberg's Hegelianism and his annoyance at an uncomprehending review of *Repetition*, he was a genuine admirer of Heiberg's dramatic work, appreciating his original plays as well as his adaptations of the French theatre.

Kierkegaard's early enthusiasm for the theatre was already apparent in the essay on Scribe's *Les Premières Amours* in the first volume of *Either/Or*, whilst Constantine's stay in Berlin (in *Repetition*) included a detailed account of his visit to the theatre and an analysis of the dramatic art of two well-known actors of the time. Kierkegaard's *Journals* show that he continued to interest himself in the theatre. Although his admiration for Shakespeare (whom he read and heard only in translation) is understandable, it is perhaps more surprising to observe his predilection for Scribe. Scribe, however, was one of the most popular dramatists of the time and between 1829 and 1855 (the period of Kierkegaard's interest in the theatre) there were no fewer than nine hundred performances of his works.[12] In his earlier years Kierkegaard had been drawn towards Scribe's satirical treatment of Romantic themes and later on he paid particular attention to the social comedies. As Kierkegaard himself was becoming increasingly hostile to worldly values, he took pleasure in Scribe's critical portrayal of society.

At first Kierkegaard had considerable doubts about the wisdom of publishing *The Crisis*, even though he was being strongly pressed by the journalist Gjødwad, who wanted it for *The Fatherland*. His increasing preoccupation with his role as a religious writer made him worry about the possible effect of such a piece upon his readers. However, after anxious inner debate, he finally allowed the essay to appear. Shortly afterwards, he was put into a similar state of uncertainty by a publisher's request for a second edition of his first major work – *Either/Or*. Once again, Kierkegaard had to ask himself whether his activity as a religious author was consistent with a return to aesthetic themes, but he finally allowed a new edition to appear, its secular emphasis being counterbalanced by the simultaneous publication (in May 1849) of 'Three Godly Discourses', *The Lilies of the Field and the Birds of the Air*.

One interesting aspect of the new edition of *Either/Or* was Kierkegaard's decision to send copies to the leading writers of the time. At this stage of his career he did not feel that such a gesture would give the impression that he was trying to create a 'coterie' for his book.[13] Even Hans Andersen was not forgotten on this occasion and on May 15 he sent Kierkegaard a short but effusive letter of thanks in which he expressed his joyful surprise that he could still be the object of such friendly thoughts.[14]

Another writer who became interested in Kierkegaard at this time was the Swedish woman-novelist Fredrika Bremer (1801–65) who

tried to meet him when she was in Copenhagen in 1849. Kierkegaard politely but firmly refused to see her.[15] His *Journals* show that
he was not unmindful of her love-affairs, for he did not hesitate to
affirm that she 'had had sexual intercourse with the notables and also
wanted to have sexual intercourse with me!'[16] Later on, in her book
Life in the North, Fredrika Bremer devoted a few pages to Kierkegaard to whom she attributed a large following of women-readers in
Copenhagen. In a more personal way she mentioned his hyper-
sensitivity to direct sunlight as a sign of psychological abnormality.
This provoked Kierkegaard to remark in his *Journals* that it was a
fine world (in Denmark) when only 'Magister Kierkegaard was
sickly and oversensitive'.[17]

Meanwhile, Kierkegaard had still not given up all idea of entering
the Church. In order to resolve the problem, he tried to see Bishop
Mynster. At first he did not find him at home; when on 25 June
Mynster agreed to see him, he gave him no more than a cordial
greeting, calling him 'dear friend', patting him on the shoulder and
then sending him away with the excuse that there was no time for a
conversation that day. As one of his biographers observes,[18] Kierkegaard was probably more relieved than disappointed by the inter-
view, for he might well have received some quite unacceptable
proposal. At least he had the satisfaction of knowing that he had
tried to do his duty by consulting the bishop about his personal
situation.

More important than this incident was Kierkegaard's desire to
clear up misunderstandings about the meaning of his work, as he
began to ponder once again the significance of his entire authorship.
Although the long essay in the *Postscript* had already reviewed his
earlier works, he obviously felt the need to re-examine the essential
nature of his production and the purpose behind it. The result was
The Point of View of my work as an author written for the most part
in 1848: in this autobiographical essay Kierkegaard stressed the
consistent religious purpose animating his whole work and at the
same time he acknowledged that his contemporaries' involvement in
false values made it necessary for him to dispel their illusions by
indirect means; the precise object of the pseudonymous writings had
been 'to deceive people into the truth'; feeling himself to be inspired
by 'divine governance', he had made it his main task to teach people
what it meant to become a Christian. 'So it is I understand myself
in my activity as an author. It makes the illusion of Christendom
evident and opens the eyes to what it is to become a Christian'.

In spite of the importance of *The Point of View* Kierkegaard felt
that it could not be published in his life-time. He excluded from this
decision an excerpt of some twenty pages, 'On my Work as an
Author', which appeared in 1851.

Meanwhile, Kierkegaard felt a need to discuss his work with some-
body who would be intelligent enough to understand it and yet
modest enough to interpret it to a wider public without distorting
its meaning by the intrusion of his own ideas. For a time, he thought
he had found such a man in the person of Rasmus Nielsen, Professor
of Philosophy at Copenhagen and the occupant of a chair which he
himself had at one time thought of seeking.[19]

I drew Rasmus Nielsen into my intimacy, because I looked upon it as my religious duty, so that there should be *at least one man*, so that it could not be said that I had overlooked the human factor.[20]

At first, Nielsen's cooperation seemed to augur well for this decision; he had shown a genuine sympathy for Kierkegaard's work and had been influenced by it to the point of giving up his attachment to Hegelianism. For a time, Nielsen shared Kierkegaard's intimacy, went for walks with him and discussed his ideas. Kierkegaard, however, soon recorded his disappointment. When Nielsen published his own book *Christian Faith and the Modern Mind* in May 1849, he did not make that open and unmistakable declaration of support for Kierkegaard which the latter had secretly – and perhaps unreasonably – expected. Already in 1849, Kierkegaard had written in his *Journals*:

> He cannot of course be very much use to me; he is too heavy, too thick-skinned, too corrupted by the age of Christian VIII. If I were to become worldly he would of course be useful. I have had to make him keep his distance, otherwise he gossips about my work in a friendly sort of way, and it must either be strung to a high pitch or hidden in complete silence.[21]

Perhaps it would have been impossible for a much more gifted and sensitive man than Nielsen to have satisfied Kierkegaard's demands. As it was, Nielsen seems to have been diverted from his role as a simple expounder of Kierkegaard's ideas by his desire to make this exposition an occasion for criticizing the contemporary theologian Martensen. In any case, the disciple soon became dissatisfied with his subordinate role; he was made angry and impatient by the master's rebukes, and finally suggested the end of their collaboration. It was in 1850 that Kierkegaard finally admitted his disappointment at the conclusion of their relationship. As Hohlenberg points out, he may not have been sorry to lose a disciple who did not measure up to his exacting demands, and henceforth he was to remain the sole expounder of his own ideas, accepting his position as an 'exception' who could not be identified with any person or party. Indeed, the publication of *Training in Christianity* in September 1850 made it clear that he was to extend little sympathy to established institutions, however exalted, and that his relations with his contemporaries were to become increasingly difficult.

Kierkegaard's literary and religious preoccupations did not prevent him from continuing to think about Regine. Although she was now married, he still hoped for some kind of reconciliation. One insuperable obstacle was the persistent refusal of her father, Councillor Olsen, to have anything to do with him. When one day, in the street, Kierkegaard tried to engage the Councillor in conversation, he was severely rebuffed. In June 1849, however, Councillor Olsen died – almost at the time when Kierkegaard was trying to decide whether to publish *The Sickness Unto Death* under his own name. The hope of renewing contact with Regine may have been one of his reasons for attributing the work to a pseudonym ('Anti-Climacus').

The night after Olsen's death, Kierkegaard had a disturbing experience: he thought he heard a voice (which he subsequently realized was his own) speaking to him:

> I was greatly overtaxed and slept rather restlessly; and strangely enough there occurred to me a word which made me feel as if I were about to plunge to destruction.[22]

Later on, he gave details of this 'conversation':

> So then it is this that is required of me? What does he imagine? I could well wait eight days. See, now he wills his own destruction.[23]

Ever his own self-analyst, he realized that the experience was due to strain and tension.

A few months later, he considered the possibility of approaching Regine once more; he was still worried about the bad impression created by his earlier behaviour.

> It would satisfy my pride to give her the greatest possible redress; it would give me pleasure to express my faithfulness; and religiously, it would be in favour of my cause – my life would become affecting.[24]

At last he decided to write to her in order to proffer 'reconciliation'. Thinking it improper to send the letter to her directly, he tried to forward it through her husband, Fritz Schlegel, with a note expressing the hope that 'a little clarification concerning my relationship to her might now be of service to her'. Schlegel refused to give his wife the letter and returned it to Kierkegaard unopened, so that this attempt to draw closer to Regine came to nought. Henceforth, Kierkegaard was to obtain no more than an occasional glimpse of her in the street. A few years later, in 1855, Schlegel was appointed to the post of governor in the Danish West Indies. In March of that years, Kierkegaard and Regine again saw each other in the street and as she passed, she said quietly to him: 'God bless you. May it go well with you'. Kierkegaard simply raised his hat without speaking. He was never to see her again.[25]

9 Despair

The Sickness Unto Death of 1849 deals with a theme already discussed in *The Concept of Dread*, but now transposed into a specifically religious key. This religious purpose is already indicated by Kierkegaard's new pseudonym, 'Anti-Climacus', the meaning of which is explained in the *Journals*, where he points out that his pseudonyms express points of view lower or higher than that of his own personal existence.

> The pseudonym is called Johannes Anti-Climacus in contrast to Johannes Climacus who said he was not a Christian. Anti-Climacus is the opposite extreme, being a Christian in an extraordinary degree – whereas I manage only to be quite a simple Christian.[1]

Whereas *Dread* deals with an area of experience preceding the emergence of freedom, the despair analysed in *The Sickness Unto Death* is a specifically spiritual phenomenon, for the individual has already expressed his freedom by choosing to exist in a sinful way. Nevertheless, Kierkegaard is still interested in the human as well as the religious aspects of the problem, as his sub-title indicates – 'a Christian psychological exposition for edification and awakening'.

In the preface to the work, Kierkegaard stresses the consequences of 'this Christian heroism' which 'is to venture wholly to be oneself, as an individual man, alone before the face of God, alone in this tremendous exertion and this tremendous responsibility' (p. 4). The religious issue, therefore, is related very closely to 'life and the reality of personal existence'. Kierkegaard proposes to consider 'the sickness unto death' within a broad Christian context, while still examining its deeper human implications. Although, as he points out at the outset, the title is suggested by Jesus' words about Lazarus ('this sickness is not unto death': *John*, II, 4), the malady here described is of a spiritual kind – 'a despair' that imperils the existence of the soul. Unlike dread, therefore (with which it has a certain affinity), despair is not a purely psychological phenomenon preceding the emergence of sin, but a spiritual experience involving the very essence of man's inner life – his separation from God. Kierkegaard's analysis, however, relates this separation from God to man's failure to establish a proper relationship with himself and stresses its grave and far-reaching repercussions upon human existence itself; it is upon this particular problem of the self's relationship with its own being that the book places its main emphasis.

In order to clarify the false relationship created by despair, Kierkegaard begins by summarily defining the nature of the human personality as 'spirit'. The earlier works, however, had already shown that the personality could not be interpreted as a static homogeneous substance (like a physical object), but only as a being that was constantly striving, through the exercise of freedom, to fulfil its highest possibilities. Since the paradoxes and tensions involved in this expression of freedom as 'becoming' concern man's existence as a synthesis of the finite and the infinite, the temporal and the eternal, it is in the disruption of this relationship that the true source of despair is to be found.

Despair may assume two main forms, although there is also a third and fairly superficial kind which is typical of the man who remains indifferent to his own personal reality; this is not genuine despair, for it lacks a truly conscious element. Genuine despair, on the other hand, either involves a deliberate refusal to be oneself, a defiant clinging to the finite and temporal and, consequently, a repudiation of the authentic spiritual possibilities of the personality, or else it is expressed as an attitude that goes no further than a merely reflective or imaginative acceptance of spiritual reality. To avoid despair it is necessary for the self to establish a relationship which allows the temporal element to take its meaning from the eternal. The presence of the eternal in the personality means that human existence cannot be adequately understood in terms of its purely finite elements but must be ultimately grounded in God – in a 'power' greater than itself, in a transcendent reality. Despair arises from the deliberate repudiation of this essential relationship and so from the misuse of freedom.

The potential reader of *The Sickness Unto Death* should not be deterred by the difficult and abstract early pages dealing with the problem of self-relationship. As the work develops, it is clear that Kierkegaard has the Christian experience very much in mind and is anxious to bring the whole question back to the point already indicated in the Preface – the reality of personal existence and its relationship to life. In any case, as soon as he has dealt with the main elements of despair, Kierkegaard goes on to describe in some remarkable pages the 'forms of this sickness', which he treats as a prominent and persistent feature of human existence. Although despair is the 'sickness unto death', there is a sense in which man's spirit is indestructible; he may seek to ignore his spiritual nature or ill-treat it, but he cannot annihilate it. Man 'cannot consume himself, cannot get rid of himself, cannot become nothing'. He may indeed will to be the self which he is not and he may will to tear himself away from God, but he cannot thereby annihilate his eternal nature. 'So also', writes Kierkegaard, 'we can demonstrate the eternal in man from the fact that despair cannot consume his self, that this is precisely the torment of contradiction in despair. If there was nothing eternal in a man, he could not despair; but if despair could consume itself, there would still be no despair' (p. 30). The sickness of despair may attack man's noblest part (his spirit), but he cannot die. 'To have a self, to be a self, is the greatest concession made to man, but at the same time it is eternity's demand upon him'.

Indifference to the various forms of despair may make men overlook its universality and mistakenly believe that they are free of its influence. This occurs whenever they allow themselves to be dominated by some purely human feeling; convinced that they are happy, they fail to understand that their happiness is simply the outward sign of a spiritual despair. This was a charge which Kierkegaard frequently levelled against his age: that it lacked spirituality, that men were so satisfied with their immediate feelings that they had forgotten what it meant to be religious individuals. According to Kierkegaard, the most wasteful tragedy of human existence occurred when a man was

> so deceived by the joys of life or by its sorrows that he never became eternally and decisively conscious of himself as spirit, as self, or (what is the same thing) never became aware and in the deepest sense received an impression of the fact that there is a God, and that he, he himself, his self, exists before this God, this gain of infinity, which is never attained except through despair [p. 40].

Since despair involves both temporal and eternal elements which have to be grasped and united through an active becoming, it can never be adequately defined in terms of a single aspect of the human personality, but needs to be understood 'dialectically' as a relationship involving its two different aspects. Although the one corrective to despair, as we have seen, is for the self to be 'grounded transparently in God' (for only in this way can it avoid the distortion or mutilation of its being) it has to be aware not only of its infinite possibilities, but also of its need to relate them to the whole personality; spiritual aspiration may remain sterile if it involves no more than the imagination or the intellect, for in this way the infinite self becomes 'fantastical' or abstract and is 'volatilized more and more' (p. 46); existence becomes a 'sort of abstract sentimentality which is so inhuman that it does not apply to any person'. Any attitude which treats the infinite as a mere possibility that does not have to be fully incorporated into personal existence, can end only in 'despair'.

The opposite danger arises when the self, instead of giving rein to its infinite possibilities, deliberately contracts or narrows its existence by limiting it to the domain of the finite and temporal. 'The lack of infinitude means to be desperately narrow-minded and mean-spirited' (p. 49). Kierkegaard is here thinking of the attitude which attributes 'infinite value to the indifferent' and sees perfection in the man who has 'made a success in the world'. Instead of allowing the infinite to express itself in his existence, he has been 'ground smooth as a pebble' and made to conform to the world's standards; he remains oblivious of the 'dreadfulness' of despair, for he refuses to become conscious of himself by 'venturing in the highest sense'.

Another and less obvious form of despair is to be found under the categories of possibility and necessity, both of which are as essential to the complete self as infinity and finitude. Although possibility obviously plays a vital role in any personal existence conceived in terms of becoming and freedom, the individual may fail to understand its true significance: he may view the process of personal becoming as a merely imaginative possibility instead of striving for genuine fulfilment. As more and more things become possible, nothing is ever made actual and the self is swallowed up in the 'abyss' of its own empty possibilities. As Kierkegaard puts it, the individual, by mistaking the wish for the deed, 'becomes for himself a mirage' (p. 55).

The 'despair of necessity' occurs when a man, by accepting subjection to some form of determinism and fatalism, or by losing himself in the trivial and the materialistic, deliberately turns his back on possibility and denies that in God 'all things are possible'. Such a man lacks 'possibility' which is 'the only power to save', the 'only saving remedy'; without it 'a man cannot, as it were, draw breath', for he is without religious strength. Only through belief in spiritual possibility can the individual find an effective antidote to despair.

Kierkegaard attaches considerable importance to the relationship between despair and consciousness – 'the more consciousness, the more intense the despair'. The point is illustrated by the example of the devil's despair; the devil, being sheer spirit, expresses the maximum of despair in the form of an absolute defiance, that is, 'a defiance with no obscurity which might serve as a mitigating excuse'. At the other extreme is the minimal despair of the innocent man who 'does not even know that there is such a thing as despair' (p. 65). The 'despair which is unconscious that it is despair' is to be found especially in people who are dominated by their 'sensuous' nature: they are so absorbed in their immediate feelings and impulses that they do not wish to be torn away from their delusion; the influence of their senses and emotions is so powerful that they do not have the courage 'to venture to be spirit or to endure it'. Kierkegaard compares such people with the inhabitants of a building who would rather remain in the cellar of sensuousness than move up into the higher floor of the spirit. This type of 'innocent' despair may be found even in persons of lofty intellectual pretensions: their minds are so busy with abstract thoughts that they have no time to think about their own inner state. In spite of their lofty claims, speculative philosophers have not faced spiritual and personal reality.

Despair, therefore, is the condition of every man who has failed to express his existence as spirit, whether he is conscious of it or not; all forms of paganism (whether inside Christianity or outside), betray the same absence of an authentic God-relationship. Perhaps Christian paganism is worse than that of the ancients who, after all, did not possess an adequate conception of God; when they discussed the question of suicide, they failed to understand the most powerful argument against it – that it was a crime against God – because they were not conscious of existing before God as spirit. Nevertheless, there is an important difference between the two kinds of paganism, since ancient paganism was 'definitely oriented in the direction of spirit', whilst paganism within Christianity moves away from it, and is 'in the strictest sense, spiritlessness'.

As soon as consciousness becomes a determining factor in despair, it is obviously capable of various degrees of intensity. It may happen, for example, that a man is conscious of having a self – even a potentially spiritual self – and yet does not succeed in establishing a proper relationship with it; he refuses to be himself or else seeks to be himself in a despairing way. This occurs when a man, after losing earthly possessions through 'misfortune' or 'fate', feels himself to be overwhelmed by some aspect of the finite world; since he attributes his condition to an external force, he never reaches the point of becoming an active self, but remains imprisoned in the limited outlook of the natural world; accordingly, he bases the meaning of his existence on something outside himself, thereby shutting himself off from spiritual possibility.

When immediacy becomes imbued with reflection, the individual's attitude does not remain quite as passive as before, for he now sees that more is involved than the problem of merely outward circumstances; he realizes that he is different from his environment and that the reality of his being cannot be determined by an external criterion; nevertheless, he is still in despair, for he is bound to the finite, although this is now an aspect of his own existence. In certain cases, he may escape from the problem altogether by having recourse to social activity or some other form of distraction, but, whatever his particular way of confronting existence, the spiritual element is never allowed to break through and impel him towards faith.

Instead of despairing over the earthly in this way (whether it be located inside the self or outside), a man may despair about the eternal, but in a manner that still betrays his weakness; the despairer realizes that it is weakness to take the earthly so much to heart, but he still remains absorbed in his unhappy feelings instead of moving on to faith; while recognizing that he is in despair over the eternal, he has not the strength to escape from his despairing mood. Admittedly, his despair has progressed to some extent, but his attitude is still spiritually barren, for he merely contemplates his situation without making a serious effort to transform it.

At this point Kierkegaard introduces a form of despair which has particular relevance to himself and is obviously connected with a theme already examined in *The Concept of Dread*. The condition of the individual who has become a victim of 'morbid reserve' is a persistent theme in many of Kierkegaard's works and, as we have seen, betrays a strongly personal preoccupation. The melancholy man locks himself up in his secret inner life, concealing from men, with whom in other respects he may be on excellent terms, what really concerns him. The self-immured individual is in despair because he cannot break through to the eternal; although his love of solitude may indicate a spiritual concern, this remains inactive and 'gets no further than the admission of its own weakness'. The way to faith has been blocked by pride, for despair over weakness has taken the form of spiritual defiance.

With the appearance of defiance the condition of despair is changed, for the individual is no longer the weak person who does not want to be himself, but one whose 'despairing abuse of the eternal' makes him determined to be himself in the wrong way (p. 108). At this stage, self-consciousness is greatly intensified and despair comes from within the self, not from outside, as in the case of despair over the earthly. The infinite self now emerges, but only in an abstract form, and in a way that divides the personality into two parts: there is a concrete self, with definite faculties and dispositions and also as a kind of negative, infinite self; the individual's error is to treat the infinite self as something apart, a kind of model by which he can judge the value of his concrete self without being compelled to integrate it into his complete personality. The reason for this is his desire to be his own master, and to determine the direction of his own existence. Spiritually speaking, however, he lacks seriousness, 'for this self-relationship excludes the very factor which could make it effective – God or the Power which posited it'.

Kierkegaard then returns once again to the special case constituted by the victim of melancholy, though it is now considered more specifically in the light of the infinite rather than in purely earthly terms. In his exploration of the concrete self, the melancholy individual will perhaps stumble upon some kind of hardship – a hardship which is 'of the kind that the Christian would call a cross, a fundamental defect, it matters not' (p. 112). Although the 'negative infinite' self may wish to ignore it or dismiss it as of no importance, it is so far from being able to do so that it actually becomes enslaved by the very defect it is trying to forget. In spite of its spiritual pretensions, this despair 'will not let itself be comforted by the eternal, for it rates the earthly so highly that the eternal can be of no comfort' (p. 113). Yet this rejection of all hope of removing an earthly distress, a temporal cross, is a serious form of despair, for the 'thorn in the flesh [and we have already discussed the profoundly personal meaning of this expression for Kierkegaard] gnaws so profoundly that [the despairer] cannot abstract it' (p. 113). Being willing to accept this burden 'as it were eternally', he is offended by it, or rather makes his attitude towards it an occasion for being offended by the whole of existence. This means that he defiantly wills to be himself, and yet wants to take his cross along with him. By doing so, he turns his back on the possibility of help, 'not to speak of help by virtue of the absurd, that for God all things are possible – no, that he will not do' (p. 114). Moreover, if he will not seek help from God, he also refuses to seek help from men, preferring to be himself 'with all the tortures of hell, if so it must be'. As this form of despair becomes intensified, so does it become demoniac. The individual's whole passion is henceforth directed upon his torment with 'demoniac rage'. Taking a perverse, defiant pleasure in his pain, he is convinced that he is in the right, so that he grows afraid of the eternity which would require him to let his torment go; he does not want to be rid of his 'demoniacally infinite advantage' over other men and his proud justification for being what he is. It is himself he wills to be, but only in this spirit of demoniac defiance. 'Ah, demoniac madness! He rages most of all at the thought that eternity might get it into its head to take his misery from him!' (p. 116).

This form of despair is undoubtedly very rare and is usually encountered, says Kierkegaard, in the works of poets who give their characters this ideal demoniac dimension. (Indeed, Kierkegaard himself in his aesthetic writings had treated many of his characters in this way.) Examples of this despair, however, may appear in real life, even though they can never be recognized by any outward sign. The introverted man of hidden melancholy, who is animated by 'what one might call inwardness with a jammed lock', is perhaps

accepted by his fellow-men as a normal, sociable being. Yet this
normality is actually a sign of demoniac defiance, for the individual
uses all his energy and shrewdness to keep his despair 'shut up in
close reserve', as he makes every effort to reduce outward appearance
'to the level of indifference, to make it as unrevealing and indifferent
as possible'. It is all important for such a despairer 'to dwell in an
exterior semblance behind which it would ordinarily never occur to
anyone to look' (p. 117). This hiddenness may be something spiritual
and a device for protecting his personal reality against the world,
but it still remains demoniac, because it is a defiant rejection of
the God-relationship which alone can make the individual truly
himself.

It is characteristic of Kierkegaard that he should conclude his
description of a general spiritual condition with a detailed examination of a case that is particularly relevant to his own situation. We
have already seen a similar approach in *Either/Or* and *The Concept
of Dread*. Nevertheless, his account of the various forms of despair
is meant to emphasize the principal factor ultimately responsible for
all despair – sin. As soon as despair takes place 'before God', it
is raised to a higher power, for it is removed from the human
categories which had characterized its other forms. Yet here again
Kierkegaard begins by considering a problem that is in many ways
his own. While admitting that psychological description would be
irrelevant to these more complex cases, he pauses to consider 'the
most dialectical borderline between despair and sin, what one might
call a poet-existence in the direction of the religious' (p. 123). In his
earlier books, Kierkegaard, as we have seen, paid considerable
attention to the activity of 'the poet', for, in the contemporary
world, it is he who in many ways upholds the cause of the ideal, and
makes his inner suffering an occasion for the portrayal of the
idealistic possibilities of existence. However, instead of remaining
in the domain of the 'natural' man, the poet here considered is of a
special kind, for he has his gaze fixed on religious values. A victim
of suffering, he turns to God as his only comfort, but he 'loves his
torment and will not let it go'. Consequently, this 'poet of religious-
ness', this 'unhappy lover of the religious', will not humble himself
in faith, but, paralysed by his pain, remains content with a merely
imaginative relationship to the religious.

Moreover, he is faced with an inner conflict, as he wonders whether
he is the elect, whether the thorn in the flesh is a sign of his extraordinary mission, or whether it is simply an experience under which
he must humble himself in order to find fulfilment in the domain of
the 'universal human'.

Kierkegaard is very anxious to clarify the full significance of
despair as sin. He points out that the Socratic definition of sin as
'ignorance' lacks one essential determinant: it fails to see that sin is
not simply a lack or misapplication of knowledge but a matter of
will. Even if it were conceded that ignorance is an aspect of sin, it
would still be necessary to ask about its origin. As an ethical teacher
Socrates was undoubtedly 'the first in his class' – and Kierkegaard

never tires of praising him for this achievement – but since the Greek thinker was not acquainted with Christian values, his conception of sin was necessarily defective. Perhaps it would be truer to say that for Socrates sin (in the Christian sense) did not exist, for he lacked the revelation from God which could alone make it meaningful; from the human standpoint also, he did not realize the importance of defiant will as the source of sin. The Greek conception was essentially intellectual and presupposed that with knowledge and enlightenment, a man could not help being good. Kierkegaard insists that the modern age, with its facile approach to 'understanding' would do well to take the Socratic notion more seriously and realize what true knowledge really involves; the world would indeed benefit from a Socrates who freed it from its delusions and made it realize that knowledge, to be real, had to exert a positive influence upon existence instead of remaining an empty abstraction. A Socrates is necessary to make people ask whether they truly understand what they say they have understood – and especially what they mean when they say they are 'Christians'! It may then emerge out that their religion and philosophy do not amount to anything more than paganism. In other words,

there live perhaps a great multitude of men who labour off and on to obscure their ethical and religious understanding which would lead them out into delusions and consequences which the lower nature does not love, extending meanwhile their aesthetic and metaphysical understanding, which ethically is a distraction (p. 153).

This limitation cannot be overcome until men realize they are dependent not only on their intellect but also on their will.

However great may have been Socrates' achievement in enabling men to distinguish between understanding and ignorance – an achievement which makes him the 'grand master of ironists' – it is impossible to remain satisfied with his standpoint, for he does not throw real light on the distinction between not being *able* to understand and not being *willing* to understand. Christianity impels us to go further and to consider the role of the defiant will: a man's failure to understand is due to his misuse of will – a fact which changes the whole meaning of his situation, for whereas comprehension is essentially a human operation, willing involves the divine attribute of faith and the necessity of receiving from God 'revelation to enlighten man as to what sin is and how deep it lies' (p. 155). As soon as he receives that revelation, he will realize the 'true nature of sin as despair over oneself "before God"'. Sin, therefore, is not a mere negation, or a simple lack of knowledge, but a positive act of will, resulting from the misuse of human freedom.

Unlike the broken, discontinuous nature of the aesthetic life, true spiritual development involves continuity. It is a law of the spiritual life that it can never remain where it is, but must always be in movement. Man cannot simply remain in sin and assume that his sin will stay as it is; as long as he does not 'get out of sin', it will continue to grow; to remain in sin is to increase it and develop 'its positive

G

continuity'. This is much worse than being guilty of particular sins, for it involves a deeper conception of sin: it is 'sin emphatically'. In the spiritual sphere, the same law applies to belief, for the 'rubric of the spirit' gives 'consistency in something higher, at least in idea'. The believer, therefore, fears the introduction of chaos and disorder into his existence, for he does not wish to be wrenched away from the totality of his spiritual life or the consistency of the good. In stressing the continuity and consistency of sin, Kierkegaard once again returns to the theme of the 'demoniac'. The demoniac man is like the drunkard whose fear of the possible consequences of sobriety explains his continual need of intoxication; he clings to the consistent totality of evil, for he realizes that goodness would loosen the grip of sin; it is this persistence in sin which holds him together and allows him to be himself. Yet by abiding in sin, he intensifies it; he exists in 'the inward direction, in more and more intense consciousness' which serves only to keep him still more closely imprisoned in the thraldom of evil.

There remain two other possible developments of despair, which are much closer to a specifically religious conception of sin since they are directly related to the figure of Christ. The self is face to face with Christ whom it knows can forgive sins, but it deliberately turns away from him, thus being no longer guilty of mere weakness or indifference but of deliberate defiance; the individual now refuses to be himself and to accept himself as a sinner. This is 'the sin of despairing of the forgiveness of sins'. The sinner rejects the 'thou shalt' which is at the heart of the Christian message, because he is offended by the idea that Christ can forgive sins. 'A specially high degree of lack of spirit is required, if one is not a believer, to take offence that a man claims to forgive sins'. Nor can the sinner escape from the problem by living in close relations which others, by losing himself in a mass of human beings or by having recourse to the consoling security of some form of philosophical idealism. Offence is inseparable from the consciousness that there is 'an infinite yawning gap' between man and God, an absolute qualitative difference which man himself can never overcome by his own efforts but which God alone can bridge by his grace. The choice is simple: to believe or to be repelled – to accept God or to take offence.

The final stage of despair is reached when man reacts to sin by a positive renunciation of Christianity, which he declares to be untruth. This is the highest form of sin, for it is a deliberate repudiation of God, 'the sin against the Holy Ghost'. Kierkegaard illustrates his point by a military metaphor: the first form of despair (neglect or indifference) tries to deal with the question of sin through 'evasive tactics'; the second simply 'holds its ground', for it remains firmly attached to sin in a negative, passive way, refusing to make an active effort to free itself; the third – the sin of abandoning Christianity and of declaring it to be falsehood – 'moves into the attack' and 'takes the offensive' against God.

We are thus brought back to the notion of offence and to the 'dialectical' element which lies in everything Christian: God prevents man from coming too near to Him, and yet, by that very means, He draws man to Himself. The human reaction to the qualitative gap between God and man once again refers the whole question to the religious existence of the individual. Despair involves a spiritual failure and the misuse of freedom. Man is responsible for the disruption of a self-relationship which can have true meaning only when it exists before God.

10 Last Years

The strongly Christian emphasis of the closing sections of *The Sickness Unto Death* had already been anticipated by the publication of the *Christian Discourses* in April 1848; in this work Kierkegaard categorically affirmed that Christianity meant 'staking all upon uncertainty' and 'venturing far out' into the unknown; Christian faith involved a personal encounter made in 'fear and trembling' and without the deceptive security of rational belief; the decisive importance of the personal relationship dispensed with any need to produce a defence or proof of the truth of Christianity. 'This personal concern, this fear and trembling as to whether a man is himself a believer, is the best remedy against all doubt about the truth of the doctrine' (p. 198). In the works and journals of this period Kierkegaard places ever increasing stress upon the antithesis between Christianity and worldly values. If necessary, the Christian must be prepared to suffer martyrdom for his belief. The challenging, almost aggressive quality of Christianity was henceforth to be given greater and greater prominence in Kierkegaard's writings. Even though he continued to call himself a poet in the service of a religious ideal, an author who wrote 'without authority', he did not hesitate to affirm the absolute nature of the Christian demand upon the individual and the inescapable obligations imposed on anyone who sought to become a Christian.

This movement towards an absolute religious standpoint was certainly accelerated by the tensions of Kierkegaard's inner life. Ever since *The Corsair* incident, he had been driven more and more into himself and made to feel the power of an all-consuming religious demand which would put him at odds not only with the world but also with the established Church. Moreover, the *Journals* continue to reveal the psychological cost of his renunciation of Regine: he could not forget what it had meant in terms of possible peace and fulfilment. For a time, as we have seen, he longed for reconciliation, in spite of her marriage, but the failure of his efforts to draw closer to her left him with nothing but the memory of what might have been had he attempted to live 'by virtue of the absurd'.

Another source of unhappiness was the inescapable influence of his melancholy. Although he found relief in his efforts to think his unhappy thoughts 'before God', he could not talk to others about them. Admittedly, he found considerable consolation in literary production. 'After a certain time has gone by, the abcess bursts – and underneath lies the richest and most beautiful material for work, and of the very kind I need at the moment.'[1] Yet, his growing preoccupation with absolute religious values often made him worry about the publication of each new work, although he eventually decided that he could satisfy both duty and desire by his direct attack upon contemporary values.

It was natural that this preoccupation with religious absolutes should ultimately bring Kierkegaard into conflict not only with official Christianity but also with revivalist movements of a less orthodox kind. He made Nikolai Grundtvig (1783–1872) the target of constant criticism: all noise and no substance was the burden of the charge Kierkegaard levelled against him in 1849.[2] Ten years earlier he had dismissed Grundtvig's famous preaching as nothing more than 'a weekly evacuation', and in 1844 he had remarked: 'He thinks that by talking he can produce a great effect. Perhaps he could produce the same effect by standing on his head'.[3] Kierkegaard thought that Grundtvig's appeal to the emotions would be more likely to produce confusion and misunderstanding than genuine spiritual conviction. Furthermore, the revivalists's plea for toleration and the freedom to proclaim his version of the Christian message without any interference from civil or ecclesiastical authorities met with very little sympathy from Kierkegaard, who considered that the Grundtvigians had failed to understand the true character of the Christian position; instead of making men aware of Christianity, they had merely made them indifferent to it. Kierkegaard was certainly unjust to Grundtvig whose preaching and hymn-writing had done much to stimulate a sense of Christian brotherhood, but it is interesting to observe how Kierkegaard's preoccupation with the individual's absolute relation to God made him hostile to a more emotional, social approach to Christianity.

Kierkegaard's criticism of Grundtvig is in striking contrast to his admiration for another defender of Christianity whose work he began to study at this time – Blaise Pascal.[4] Kierkegaard saw in Pascal a thinker who tried to re-establish an honest radical religion in an age of false values, and consequently, to free men from the illusion of 'Christendom'. Moreover, Pascal, in Kierkegaard's view, was not content to denounce dishonesty and hypocrisy; he sought also to explain the nature of true faith – how it depends on the appropriation of religious truth into the reality of personal experience, of 'reduplicating' in the individual himself what he – and others – profess as true religion. When judged by the standards of the world, Christianity may seem a hard and paradoxical religion, but this is largely due to the nature of its revelation which, strangely enough, can be communicated only through its opposite – concealment. To both Pascal and Kierkegaard it was important for men to understand the meaning of the spoken words and concepts they use in their religious life. The recognition of this fact may cause many people to be 'offended' by Christianity. But in the long run this is a necessary and beneficial reaction on the part of those who seek to relate themselves absolutely to the absolute.

It was with the publication of *Training in Christianity* in 1850 that Kierkegaard threw into sharp relief the exact nature of the Christian challenge. The themes of paradox and offence, already present in *The Sickness Unto Death*, become the main object of his attention, with particular stress being placed upon their relevance to Christianity. A consideration of these themes is inseparable from the equally radical notion of 'contemporaneousness with Christ'. *Training in Christianity* goes to the very heart of Kierkegaard's conception of Christianity and at the same time begins to make very clear the basis of his opposition to the established Church. As he puts it in the preface, 'the requirement of being a Christian is strained by the pseudonym [Anti-Climacus] to the highest pitch of ideality'. The demands of true Christianity must be 'uttered, plainly set forth and heard'; no compromise is possible with a religion that makes absolute demands upon both the individual and the Church. It is this essential point which gives *Training in Christianity* its radical character, and explains why in his last years Kierkegaard saw himself more and more as a writer whose task was to make men aware of their false conception of Christianity.

Kierkegaard believed that the modern world was making a grave error in wanting to adapt Christianity to its own corrupt and meretricious standards; more especially, it was trying to make Christ acceptable to man by eliminating his lowly role as a despised servant and by presenting him in a falsely idealized light. Kierkegaard also rejected those historical and rational interpretations of Christ's life and personality which tried to make them seem more comprehensible to the human mind. Christ, he affirmed, could not be sentimentalized or rationalized in this way. The dilution or distortion of Christian values was usually prompted by an attempt to avoid giving offence to feeling and reason, but, in Kierkegaard's view, offence could be removed from Christianity only at the cost of destroying it as a living faith. It was because Christianity disturbed normal complacency and security that the individual had to make it a part of his inner life.

What, then, does being 'contemporaneous with Christ' mean? It obviously cannot involve an attempt to return, through some kind of imaginative or historical reconstruction, to Christ's original situation; nor can it mean modernizing Christ in a way that makes him amenable to the outlook of the contemporary world; 'to be contemporaneous with Christ' does not mean establishing a merely temporal or historical relationship with him. When Christ says 'Come unto me', he is not thinking of physical proximity in space and time; he is exhorting men to draw near in faith, which, in turn, is possible only in spiritual terms and through a radical transformation of their inner lives. That is why they are either attracted to or offended by the absolute demand made upon them.

Being 'contemporaneous with Christ' becomes all the more difficult when He appears to us in the guise of a humble servant, and not as an awesome divine figure; our immediate impulse is to reject him as unworthy of his claim to be God. Yet as soon as we are truly contemporaneous with Christ, we perceive the deeper meaning of the absolute spiritual demand; it is God who wants our salvation by presenting himself to us in this way, and it is God who permits of no compromise; it is men – and the Church – who have sought to weaken Christianity by adapting it to purely human ideals and making it something other than what it truly is. 'Christianity did not come into the world (as the parsons snivellingly and falsely introduce it) as an admirable example of the gentle art of consolation – but as the *absolute*. It is out of love that God wills it so, but also it is *God* who wills it. He wills what He will' (p. 66). God will not let himself be changed into a 'nice, human God'; it is he who requires men to transform themselves into spiritual beings by meeting with faith the challenge of his paradoxical revelation of himself.

The existence of the God-Man, the possibility of offence and the need for faith are the three essential constituents of Christianity:

> For this is the law: he who has done away with faith has done away with the possibility of offence (as when speculation substitutes comprehension for faith); and he who does away with the possibility of offence does away with faith (as when the languishing sermon of the parson mendaciously attributes to Christ direct recognizeableness). But whether one does away with faith or with the possibility of offence, one does away at the same time with something else – the God-Man. And if one does away with the God-Man, one does away with Christianity [p. 143].

It would be misleading to suggest that the whole of *Training in Christianity* is written in the stern, challenging spirit of the section dealing with the notion of offence. The concluding part ('From on high he will draw all men unto himself') is composed in a more meditative mood, even though it in no way diminishes the absoluteness of the Christian requirement. Christ will not 'entice' men but 'draw' all to Himself. Yet this act of 'drawing all' to him means presenting them with a choice and, consequently, with the need to exercise their freedom. Yet as soon as a man uses his freedom in this way he realizes that his life has to give reality to his faith and that the perfection he apprehends in Christ has to become part of his own existence and be expressed 'day after day by the actual sufferings of reality'. 'Life's seriousness consists in the *will* to be and to express perfection (ideality) in everyday reality'. Truth, therefore, does not consist in knowing but in being, and, if necessary, in experiencing deep suffering. Unlike the admirer who simply stands aloof, the follower of Christ strives to be what he admires. Without this essential condition all attempts to be a Christian are fruitless.

The Sickness Unto Death (1849) and *Training in Christianity* (1850) were followed by two more serious works, *For Self-Examination* (1851) and *Judge for Yourselves* (1851–2), only the first of which was published in Kierkegaard's life-time. They give much greater prominence to the polemical elements already present in *Training in Christianity* and challenge the age to examine the whole basis of its religious outlook; once again Kierkegaard emphasizes the uncompromising demands of true Christian faith. He seeks above all to clear away the confusions and misunderstandings of a world that seeks to adapt Christianity to its own purposes instead of accepting it in all its rigour. It becomes increasingly apparent also that Kierkegaard is anxious for the Church to admit its own deficiencies and so transform itself into a worthy vehicle for the Christian religion; only in this way can it be freed from its abject submission to the values of the 'world'.

Training in Christianity should not be considered in isolation from the other Christian writings which are far from having the fierceness of a work that was already influenced by a strong polemical purpose.

The more consoling side of the Christian faith is already discernible in the *Works of Love* (1847) and in the *Christian Discourses* (1848) and had it not been for his bitter quarrel with the Church, Kierkegaard might well have gone on to develop still further this aspect of Christianity.

At first Kierkegaard's potential aggression against the Church was held in check by his respect for its leading representative – Bishop Mynster. Although Kierkegaard was already convinced that Mynster was trying to 'deify the established order and in his zeal for morality identify it with what is bourgeois', he could not attack him openly. One reason for his restraint was the knowledge of what Mynster had meant to his father. On his side the bishop was showing an increasing hostility to Kierkegaard; he criticized *Training in Christianity* (1850) as a 'profane game with the holy'. It was more and more apparent that Mynster and Kierkegaard personified diametrically opposed attitudes: on the one side stood the supreme representative and defender of the established ecclesiastical order, and, on the other, the solitary individual who felt impelled to challenge it in the name of the 'extraordinary'.

Kierkegaard's sense of isolation was intensified by his growing awareness that he stood for religious principles which were beyond the grasp of his contemporaries. He felt that 'people are completely ignorant of what Christianity is; that is why I am left without sympathy, that is why I am not understood at all'.[5] An important entry in the *Journals* sums up his position: 'My standpoint. I delineate Christianity. For that purpose I have all the requirements in an unusual degree, and consider that to be, quite literally, my calling, to which I have been led in the most curious way from my earliest years.'[6] 'The category of my work', he said in another entry, '*is to make men aware* of Christianity'.[7]

As the defender of Christianity, Kierkegaard was increasingly critical of the official Lutheranism of his day. While admitting that Lutheranism had been a necessary corrective to the errors of Roman Catholicism, Kierkegaard believed that the corrective had been substituted for the true religion, and that 'if it claims independently to be the whole of Christianity, it brings forth the subtlest kind of worldliness and paganism'.[8] In his view, the only way to shake men from their complacent acceptance of this inadequate religion which failed to understand the meaning of true spiritual endeavour, was to introduce the notion of 'the imitation of Christ'. Kierkegaard was convinced that his own exceptional position and talents qualified him to do this, but 'without authority', for 'this is and remains my category'.[9]

Kierkegaard was henceforth convinced that Christianity could not be achieved without personal suffering. 'Little by little I have noticed more and more that all those who have really loved God . . . have all had to suffer in this world. Further, that this is the doctrine of Christianity: to be loved by God and to love God is to suffer'. This meant that Christianity must be a call to asceticism and not to the 'enjoyment of his life'. This was a point to which Kierkegaard gave ever increasing stress in his last years. He also began to realize the implications of his own particular position and task.

There are men whose qualification is to be sacrificed, in one way or another, sacrificed for others in order to forward the idea – and with my particular cross, I was such a man.[10]

Although he was still aware of his melancholy and the persistence of the 'thorn in the flesh', he began to feel a sense of fulfilment. On 13 February 1853 he wrote:

I now feel so happy, so rich, so indescribably rich, at the present time, I really am, had I to describe it, like a man who has received enormous riches, at the moment when he does not even want to think about the individual riches, basks in the whole of it – indeed I am infinitely richer.[11]

A decisive event occurred on 30 January 1854, with the death of the aged Bishop Mynster. This was a prelude to the last and most violent phase of Kierkegaard's life. The *Journals* for 1 March of that year record his reactions: 'So now he is dead. If only it had been possible for him to end his life with the admission that what he represented was not really Christianity, but a mitigation of it; for he carried a whole age along with him'.[12] By refusing to confess that he did not represent true spirituality, he 'had hardened Christianity into a deception'.

The event which sparked off Kierkegaard's indignation was the commemorative service for Bishop Mynster which took place on the Sunday (5 February) before his funeral; Professor H. L. Martensen preached a eulogistic sermon in which he claimed that the dead bishop had been a 'genuine witness to the truth', and 'a link in the holy chain of witnesses to the truth which stretches through the ages from the days of the apostles'. Kierkegaard immediately composed a vigorous refutation of this claim, but held back its publication until 18 December when it appeared in the daily paper *The Fatherland*. Kierkegaard had also noted in his *Journals* that if Mynster was a true witness, then Christianity did not exist, or existed only in a very unreal sense.

His article took up the same theme with its challenging title: 'Was Bishop Mynster a "witness to the truth", one of "the genuine witnesses to the truth" – is this the truth?'[13] Kierkegaard answered his own questions by pointing out that Bishop Mynster 'soft-pedals, slurs over, suppresses, omits something decisively Christian, something which appears to us men inopportune, which would make our life strenuous, hinder us from enjoying life, that part of Christianity which has to do with dying from the world, by voluntary renunciation, by hating oneself, by suffering for the doctrine'.[14] Moreover, Kierkegaard insisted that the bishop's personal life was marked by none of the suffering and torment which was the lot of the true witness. Compared with the true witness who suffers for his beliefs, Mynster emerged as a man who was 'shrewd to a high degree, but weak, self-indulgent and only great as a declaimer'.

Martensen published a rejoinder in which he rejected Kierkegaard's excessively narrow definition of a 'witness' and denied that such a person need suffer physical danger; each man had to be a

Christian according to his own particular capacity and talents and that is what Mynster had been. In the latter part of his reply he questioned the sincerity of Kierkegaard's intention and even accused him of being disloyal to his father's memory by launching such an attack. Kierkegaard did not find many defenders, but his former 'disciple', Rasmus Nielsen, supported him in an article in *The Fatherland* on 10 January, and spoke of his 'good deed'. Kierkegaard himself does not seem to have paid much heed to either praise or blame. Having once started his attack, he was soon to broaden it out and direct it upon the whole of the established Church.

Ten days later Kierkegaard published another article in which he reaffirmed and amplified the argument of the first, asserting that 'compared with the Christianity of the New Testament, the Mynsterish preaching and ecclesiastical rule (if it would not make the admission, and make it as solemnly as possible, that it was not the Christianity of the New Testament) was an illusion of the senses'; 'it did not resemble even in the remotest way' the Christianity of the New Testament, which involved 'the very deepest and most incurable breach with the world'. Soon the attack was turned against Mynster's panegyrist, Martensen, who was alleged to have transformed the whole Church Establishment, Christianly understood, into 'an impudent indecency' by his misrepresentation of Mynster as a 'witness of the truth'. With each article Kierkegaard's voice became more intense and strident. By the time he had reached his eighth contribution he was ready to state 'what must be done – whether by me or another': 'First and foremost, and on the greatest possible scale, an end must be put to the whole official – well-meaning – falsehood which well-meaningly conjures up and maintains the illusion that what is preached is Christianity, the Christianity of the New Testament'. Here was a case in which 'no quarter must be given'. As for his own role, he repudiated any suggestion that he was a 'reformer' or 'a profoundly speculative spirit, a seer, a prophet'; he was only 'a poet' and an 'accomplished detective talent' eager to track down falsehood and hypocrisy.

Kierkegaard moved on to condemn 'Protestantism, especially in Denmark' as 'an untruth, a piece of dishonesty, which falsifies the teaching, the world-view, the life-view of Christianity, just as soon as it is regarded as a principle for Christianity, not as a remedy at a given time and place' (p. 34). In spite of his violent attack upon Protestantism, Kierkegaard denied that he had any intention of entering the Roman Catholic Church, for this, he affirms, would be a 'precipitate act which I shall not commit, but which perhaps people will expect, since in these times it is as though it were entirely forgotten what Christianity is, and even those who have the best understanding of Christianity are only types'. In spite of his increasing tendency to contrast Protestantism unfavourably with certain aspects of Roman Catholicism, Kierkegaard remained to the end a staunch defender of Christian individualism and it is doubtful whether he could ever have reconciled it with Roman Catholic authoritarianism. 'No,' he affirmed in the eleventh article, 'one can well be alone in being a Christian'. If this meant a drastic reduction in the number of true Christians, then there was no need to be afraid of drawing the appropriate conclusion: 'the fewer the better' (p. 34).

By 31 March he had reached his twelfth article in which he asked the important question: 'What do I want?' His answer was straightforward. 'Quite simply: I want honesty.' He re-affirmed the absolute antithesis between 'the ordinary Christianity of the land' and the Christianity of the New Testament and was particularly scathing in his contempt for the paid ministers who let financial considerations stifle the true Christian requirement. Any attempt to equate true religion with the making of money would be 'a sly death-blow to Christianity'.

The twentieth article was prompted by a new edition of *Training in Christianity* and at the end of it Kierkegaard returned once more to the subject of Mynster, explaining that it was out of consideration for him that the book did not contain a direct attack on the Establishment. He was sure, however, that the old bishop had seen the book as an attack upon the Church, even though 'he impotently chose to do nothing, except at the most to condemn it in the drawing-room'.[15] The twenty-first and last article was accompanied by a vigorous pamphlet entitled: *This has to be said; let it now be said*, in which people were exhorted not to take part in 'the public worship of God'; they would thereby cease 'treating God as a fool' and engaging in 'counterfeit and forgery'. Kierkegaard was determined to warn his readers of the 'monstrous illusion' effected by the State and the priesthood in making people believe that 'this is Christianity'.

The cessation of the articles in *The Fatherland* was simply a prelude to the renewal of the attack in another form – a series of broadsheets entitled *The Instant*, together with another pamphlet: *What Christ's Judgement is about Christianity*. In the pamphlet Kierkegaard began by briefly reviewing his own production, explaining why he gave himself out to be a mere poet with the intention of 'aiming slyly at what I thought might well be the real situation of official Christianity – that it was a forgery', which 'does actually turn Christianity into poetry, doing away with the following of Christ'.

The ten numbers of *The Instant* express the same overriding preoccupation with the contrast between official and New Testament Christianity; the priests are constantly berated for their allegedly dishonest and hypocritical claim to be preaching true Christianity, whereas they are actually guilty of 'the most dreadful mockery'; nominal Christians are castigated with the same severity for constituting 'from generation to generation a society of non-Christians'. Kierkegaard seems to have paused only once in the course of his fierce indictment: in August 1855, he composed and published an edifying discourse, 'in memory of my deceased father, one time hosier in this city', on the subject of *The Unchangeableness of God*, the tone and style of which are more restrained and reflective than those of the pamphlets; in the unchangeableness of God there is rest and refreshing coolness for the 'thirsty traveller, the errant wanderer'.[16] It was perhaps appropriate that the last number of *The Instant* should be devoted to 'My task'. It attacked 'the knavish tradesmen, I mean the priests who by falsifying the definition of Christianity for the sake of business profits have acquired millions and millions of Christians'. Kierkegaard goes on to reaffirm for the last time his love of Socrates: 'thou noble simpleton of olden times, thou, the only *man* I admiringly recognize as teacher'. These legions of false Christians are little more than Sophists in the presence of Socrates and deserve to be treated with the same contempt. Kierkegaard's own professed ignorance of Christianity makes him draw close to the knowing ignorance of Socrates. 'I am not a Christian – and unfortunately I am able to make it evident that the others are not either, yea, even less than I.' 'My task', affirms Kierkegaard, 'is a Socratic task, to revise the definition of what it is to be a Christian' (p. 283).

At first sight, the intensity of Kierkegaard's attack, as well as its limited intellectual content, may surprise readers accustomed to the complexity and subtlety of his earlier works, but in this last phase of his life, he clearly no longer saw himself as a mere exponent of ideas but as an active and relentless opponent of established institutions – as a man making a call for deeds, not words. During this final period too, he felt an increasing personal hostility not only towards corrupt institutions but also towards the physical aspect of existence itself: his broken engagement and *The Corsair*'s campaign had driven him into himself, building up inner tensions which expressed themselves in his aversion to the world. Sincere convictions thus became intensified by the pressure of personal stress and tended to assume an exaggerated, one-sided form. His ever greater insistence upon the ascetic, other-worldly aspect of the religious life made him acutely conscious of the shortcomings of the official Church as the symbol of a supine acquiescence in worldly compromise and, consequently, of a calamitous betrayal of the Christian ideal. Likewise, his animadversions against Luther were based on the charge that the reformer and his successors had sought to introduce earthly pleasures ('girls, wine and cards') into the Christian Church, thereby excluding poverty, prayer and fasting. If the medieval Church had too readily assumed that spiritual ideals could be identified with a certain physical mode of existence, the modern world, and especially Protestantism, had swung to the opposite extreme of abolishing all distinction between the sacred and the profane and of 'setting the public on the throne'.[17]

In spite of this violent attack upon Christendom Kierkegaard continued to interest himself in philosophy and one important discovery of his last years was the work of Schopenhauer: 'unquestionably an important writer, he has interested me very much and I am astonished to find an author who, in spite of complete disagreement, touches me at so many points'.[18] On one particular issue, however, Kierkegaard had serious reservations – that Schopenhauer had failed to express his ethical teaching (especially his advocacy of asceticism) in his own life. Even so, Kierkegaard considered that Schopenhauer's work offered a radical challenge to 'the whole mean donnish racket' with its absurd 'twaddle' and false optimism; a little dose of Schopenhauer's ethic could be a very effective remedy against the 'infection' of contemporary poison.

During this period Kierkegaard seems to have withdrawn more and more into himself, shunning any formal relations with his contemporaries. In any case, his educated fellow-citizens were shocked by his attacks upon the Church and left him for the most part alone. His main contact was with people whom he met in the street and at least one contemporary reported that his personal manner was quiet and composed, and bore little resemblance to the furious passions of his inner life. Apparently, the only people who reacted favourably to his message were those of the lower classes, who, according to Frithiof Brandt, began to see in him a champion of their own claims for social justice.[19]

On 22 October 1855, Kierkegaard collapsed unconscious in the street, and was immediately taken to the Frederiks Hospital. An exact diagnosis of his illness was never made, but he seems to have suffered some kind of spinal paralysis, for he lost the use of his legs. When he recovered consciousness, he was willing to receive few visitors, and would not allow even his brother Peter to see him. An important exception was Emil Boesen, a friend of his youth who had become a pastor, and who made valuable notes of his last conversations with Kierkegaard. Some relatives, including his niece, Henriette Lund, also visited him. In spite of the gradual deterioration of his physical condition as the paralysis spread to different parts of his body, Kierkegaard's lucidity does not seem to have been impaired. His niece even mentioned a 'gleam of light' which shone forth from his dying countenance. 'Never in such a manner have I seen the spirit break through its earthly frame and lend it a radiance as if it were the glorified body at the dawn of the resurrection day'.[20] Henriette's half-brother, Troels Lund, then a boy of fifteen, who also visited the dying Kierkegaard, noticed that all his energy was concentrated in his eyes which 'shone with a soulfulness that made an indelible impression'. As the boy turned to leave, Kierkegaard gave him a look that 'streamed forth with an uplifted, glorified, blessed gleam', so that it seemed to fill the whole room with light.[21] To Boesen, Kierkegaard spoke of his task, though with none of the passion which had characterized his last publications. His 'thorn in the flesh', he said, had 'prevented him from entering into "the usual relations of life" ' and had convinced him that his task was 'extraordinary'. 'I tried to carry it out as best I could; I was the toy of Providence which produced me and I was to be used'. His 'life and fate as an extraordinary messenger' had stood in the way of his engagement. 'I did think that it could be changed, but it could not'. Asked by his friend whether he had anything to say, Kierkegaard replied:

No; yes, remember me to everyone, I was much attached to them all, and tell them that my life is a great, and to others unknown and unintelligible suffering. It all looked like pride and vanity, but it was not. I am no better than others, I said that and never anything else; I had my thorn in the flesh and so I did not marry and could take no office; for I am a theological student and had a public right and was well sponsored, so I could have had anything I wanted, but instead I became the exception. The day passed in work and effort, and in the evening I was set aside, that was the exception.[22]

To his friend's exhortation that he should take Holy Communion, Kierkegaard replied that he would receive it only from a layman, not from a priest. When told that this would be difficult, he replied: 'Then I shall die without it'. He insisted, however, that he would continue to pray for the forgiveness of his sins, and that he might be 'free from despair in death'. At moments his spirit would suddenly soar upwards as he had 'the feeling of becoming an angel, and of growing wings'; he wanted to 'sit astride a cloud and sing "Alleluia! Alleluia! Alleluia!".' Asked whether this was because he believed in Christ and flew to the grace of God, he answered: 'Yes, of course, what else?'

It was soon obvious that with the spread of his paralysis Kierkegaard would not live long and he himself refused to delude himself with any hope of recovery. One of the last questions Boesen (who was called away from Copenhagen almost immediately afterwards) asked him was: 'Did you publish the *Instants* you wanted to?' Kierkegaard replied: 'Yes'. 'What a lot in your life has come out exactly right'. 'Yes, that is why I am very happy and very melancholy, for I cannot share my happiness with anyone'.

Boesen saw his friend for the last time on 27 October, for when he returned to Copenhagen a few weeks afterwards, he found that Kierkegaard had died on 11 November.

In the years preceding his death, Kierkegaard had become increasingly worried about his financial situation. 'What really tortures me', he admits in his *Journals*, 'is the question of money'. In spite of his dwindling fortune, he had steadfastly refused to earn his living, as he believed that this would interfere with his real task. 'As long as I had a little money, it was still possible to hold out for the idea'.[23] As he lay dying, he admitted that he was 'financially ruined and had nothing left, only enough for his funeral'. His fear of poverty seems to have been well-grounded, for after his death there was just enough money to pay for the hospital expenses and the funeral. His few possessions (of which his library of 2,000 volumes was the most important) were subsequently sold by auction. The funeral was an embarrassing problem for another reason, since there were some who doubted whether such an intransigent opponent of the Church ought to be buried according to its rites. Peter Kierkegaard, whom Søren had refused to see during his last weeks, decided that the funeral would take place in the Cathedral Church of Our Lady, on 18 November, and he assumed the responsibility of delivering the oration; he spoke with tact and restraint as he tried to look beyond the conflicts of the immediate present to his brother's concern with 'the truth and gravity of eternity'. In the churchyard, Kierkegaard's nephew, the young doctor Henrik Lund, protested against the service and went on to read passages from the Bible and *The Instant* in support of his objection that a formal Christian burial would have been against the ideas and wishes of the dead man.

There was, however, no other incident and the large crowd was able to disperse in peace.

Kierkegaard left two letters addressed to his brother. The first was intended to be his will, and stipulated that 'my erstwhile fiancée, Mrs Regine Schlegel, shall inherit unconditionally all the little I possess', for he wished to indicate that 'an engagement is to me as binding as a marriage'. As soon as the Schlegels were informed of the contents of the 'will', they wrote back to Peter Kierkegaard with the request that the executors should act 'as if this "testament" had not existed'. The second letter, dated August 1851, was meant to leave posterity in no doubt concerning the personal inspiration of Kierkegaard's whole production:

> The one unnamed, whose name some day will be named – to whom all my work is dedicated, is my erstwhile fiancée, Mrs. Regine Schlegel.

In accordance with Kierkegaard's own wish, a verse by the poet Brorson, was inscribed on his grave:

> Yet a little while
> And I have won,
> Then the whole conflict
> With it has gone,
> So may I rest
> In valleys soft,
> And for ever
> Speak with Jesus.*

* The Danish original reads:

> Det er en liden tid
> sa har jeg vunden.
> Sa er den ganske strid
> med eet forsvunden.
> Sa kan jeg hvile mig
> i rosendale
> og uafladelig
> min Jesum tale.

11 Conclusion

Although the complex elements which make up the personality and work of Kierkegaard have influenced later generations in different ways, there has been fairly general agreement that he is one of the first 'modern' thinkers – the first who made a decisive break with a long-established philosophical tradition in order to portray the human condition in the light of hitherto unsuspected or neglected existential possibilities. Kierkegaard's insistence on the role of the exception and his constant appeal to 'the individual' have won for him the reputation of a thinker whose uncompromising defence of personal ideals led him to prefer loneliness and unpopularity to the comfortable security of rational principles. In his own day, as we have seen, he was the vigorous opponent of viewpoints which, in his opinion, hindered a proper understanding of human nature: after expressing a certain sympathy for Romanticism as a movement aimed at restoring poetry and imagination to a drab, materialistic world, he became increasingly aware of the dangers of indiscriminate emotions and passions which obscured the perception of essential moral and religious principles; likewise, in spite of an early interest in Hegel he fiercely attacked a metaphysical system which, by according supreme value to an all-embracing Absolute, eliminated the paradox and tension of human existence as a synthesis of the finite and the infinite, the temporal and the eternal; all forms of Romanticism and philosophical idealism, in Kierkegaard's view, tended to reduce experience to a single quality or explain it in terms of one supreme principle. In his last years too, Kierkegaard attacked a Church which, he alleged, had sacrificed true Christianity to the pursuit of worldly values, thus weakening the absolute nature of the Christian demand. In the eyes of later generations, to whom Romanticism, Hegelianism or even Christianity had ceased to be such burning issues, Kierkegaard still remained the individualist who, by staking all on a leap into the unknown, scorned the safety of universal values for the sake of discovering new possibilities of personal being.

In his bold defiance of philosophical tradition, Kierkegaard has often been compared with Nietzsche who made a similar assault on metaphysics and orthodox religion in the name of the human 'will'. Philosophy no longer remained tied to the search for some form of rational certainty, but involved the exploration of a 'dialectical' mode of consciousness that went beyond reason in order to seek the ultimate source of all values in the activity of personal choice and freedom. Freedom and personal commitment rather than reason and reflection became the source of philosophical truth. Kierkegaard thus shook philosophy out of its complacent acceptance of rational principles and took it to a realm of experience where the very foundations of thought itself were suddenly called into question.

Germany was the first major European country to have been

profoundly influenced by Kierkegaard's views. By the beginning of
the twentieth century, German philosophers and theologians were
already familiar with certain aspects of his outlook. It was, however,
through the work of the two 'philosophers of existence', Martin
Heidegger and Karl Jaspers, that Kierkegaard began to exert a
formative influence on the development of 'existentialism'. In his
famous *Being and Time* (1927) Heidegger praised Kierkegaard for
his 'existential' insight, whilst the analysis of 'dread' in the same work
obviously owed a great deal to him; the voluminous three-volume
Philosophie (1932) of Karl Jaspers praised Kierkegaard for having
shown how a man's world-view is related to the notion of possibility
and choice, and the ultimate mystery of Transcendence. It was only
later that French philosophy, and especially the 'existentialism' of
Sartre (who had also studied in Germany and was familiar with the
work of Heidegger) began to bear witness to Kierkegaard's powerful
influence. Existentialism, whether it be that of Sartre or Jaspers
(Heidegger has denied that he is an existentialist in spite of his great
impact on the movement), is a complex philosophy that has been
shaped by various influences, including the phenomenology of
Husserl, but it is clearly indebted to Kierkegaard for such fundamental notions as freedom, dread and possibility, and for the view
of man as a being whose conception of existence is derived from the
exercise of his freedom. In one very important respect, however,
existentialism – at least, in its Sartrean form – differs radically from
Kierkegaard, and that is in its rejection of the all-important qualification 'before God'. (In this matter the 'dialectical theology' of
Karl Barth and Emil Brunner is much more faithful to Kierkegaard's ideas in its stress upon the absolute transcendence of God
and the necessity of revelation). Kierkegaard would certainly have
protested very vigorously against any attempt to give his thought a
purely secular emphasis. Prophetically, he declared that his works
would be appropriated by the 'dons', made the subject of lectures
and so be thoroughly misunderstood! Although existentialists retain
for the most part Kierkegaard's conception of human nature as
tension and paradox and his insistence on the uniqueness of human
freedom, they do not accept his view of man as a synthesis of the
finite and the infinite, but seek to understand human nature in
purely finite terms. Man is thus left with the lonely and anguishing
responsibility of exercising his unique freedom in a world where he
no longer feels 'at home', and where he cannot find the consolation
of God's presence. For Kierkegaard, on the other hand, the dread
and anguish of freedom are made meaningful as soon as the individual exists 'before God'.

The tendency of existentialist thinkers to interpret man's relationship to the world in affective rather than intellectual terms has
certainly been due, in large measure, to Kierkegaard's influence.
Man's first response to the world, insists Heidegger, is one of
'concern' and it is this concern which ultimately determines his
comprehension of existence; his ultimate view of the human condition comes from his deep inner response to the totality of things.
Other existential thinkers also affirm that fundamental moods such
as *ennui*, nausea or hope are a more trustworthy source of philo-

H

sophical reflection about the universe than a method of detached intellectual analysis. Although such moods still have to be carefully analysed and related to the total structure of human experience, they are deemed to constitute the origin of all valid thought about the nature of man and his place in the world.

If, in Kierkegaard's opinion, man does not find realization in establishing a direct relationship with universal principles (even though these have value at a certain level of experience), it is because his freedom impels him towards the absolute. It is the pull of the absolute which keeps man constantly in movement and leaves him dissatisfied with merely finite achievements. As Kierkegaard puts it in *Fear and Trembling*, 'the individual is higher than the universal' and he 'determines his relation to the universal by his relation to the absolute, not his relation to the absolute by his relation to the universal'. The individual's relationship with the absolute may involve him in a profound sense of personal responsibility which overwhelms him with loneliness and anguish and leaves him floating perilously over 'seventy thousand fathoms'. No doubt this burden will be lifted as soon as he exists 'before God', but his relationship with the divine is inseparable from his strenuous efforts to become himself in a truly spiritual sense. The absolute ideal, therefore, can lead to personal fulfilment, but it can also plunge the individual into despair and make him fear the responsibility of freedom – man can know the joy of existing before God, but he can also experience the misery of separation from Him. In either case, it is not a question of a search for disinterested intellectual truth, but of a personal choice involving guilt and dread rather than blindness and ignorance. That is why Kierkegaard has been considered as a great analyst of the human condition by those who repudiate the notion of existing before God, and (in Reinhold Niebhur's words) as 'the greatest of Christian psychologists' by those who accept his dedication to the religious absolute.

The impact of Kierkegaard's work does not depend solely upon its philosophical or religious content, important though this is, but on the pervasive intimate connection between his ideas and his own sense of personal involvement in the subject-matter of his thought. Although he sought constantly to move away from the domain of limited individual experience to the wider issue of man's spiritual destiny, the powerful personal inspiration of his work served to show that any valid view of existence must be derived from the deepest recesses of a man's nature and not from a process of mere reflection. Because he considered his work to be his 'own education' and 'upbringing', he was able to penetrate deeply into the mystery of the human condition and to make later generations ask once again what it means to choose to be a human being.

Notes to Chapters

The following abbreviations are used in the notes:

S.V.: *Kierkegaards Samlede Vaerker*, 20 vols., Copenhagen, new edition, 1962–4.

Papirer: *Kierkegaards Papirer*, 22 vols., Copenhagen, new edition, 1968–70.

References are given in accordance with the convention now generally accepted by Kierkegaard scholars: volume (and part, where necessary), section and number of entry. Each volume is divided into three sections: A (Journals), B (drafts of works), C (notes on reading).

Journals: *The Journals of Søren Kierkegaard*, ed. A. Dru, Oxford, 1938. Numbered references are to entries, not pages.

Last Years: *Kierkegaard: The Last Years. Journals 1853–1855*, ed. and trans. R. Gregor Smith, London, 1965.

Breve og Akstykker: *Breve og Akstykker vedrørende S. Kierkegaard*, ed. N. Thulstrup, 2 vols., Copenhagen, 1953–4.

Journals (Hong): *Søren Kierkegaard's Journals and Papers*, Vol. I A–E; Vol. II, F–K, ed. H. V. and E. H. Hong, Bloomington–London, 1967, 1970.

Chapter 1

1 *Journals*, 754.
2 Cf. *Johannes Climacus*, p. 103, where Kierkegaard seems to be describing under a pseudonym his own relationship with his father.
3 *Journals*, 867.
4 Cf. the pseudonymous account in *Either/Or*, II, 223–4, which biographers agree represents Kierkegaard's own experience.
5 Quoted in W. Lowrie, *Kierkegaard*, Oxford, 1938, p. 57, and J. Hohlenberg, *Søren Kierkegaard* (trans. T. H. Croxall), London, 1954, p. 43.
6 'Half child-play, half God in the heart', also quoted by Lowrie, *op. cit.*, p. 58.
7 Cf. the introduction to his translation of *Johannes Climacus*, especially pp. 19–20. For the lecture see Hohlenberg, *op. cit.*, p. 66 and *S.V.*, I B2.
8 *Papirer*, IA, 15. Quoted in Hohlenberg, *op. cit.*, pp. 50–1.
9 *Op. cit.*, p. 164, where Hamann is said to be 'the only author by whom Kierkegaard was profoundly influenced'. See also the references under 'Hamann' in *Journals* (Hong), II, 199–205.
10 *Journals*, 16.
11 *Ibid.*, 20.
12 *Ibid.*, 22.

13 Most biographers situate this episode in 1835, but some scholars (e.g. K. Bruun Andersen, *Søren Kierkegaards store Jordystelser*, Copenhagen, 1953; F. Brandt, *Der junge Kierkegaard*, Copenhagen, 1924) have argued for another date, 5 May 1838, when Kierkegaard was twenty-five.

14 *Journals*, 243.

15 *Op. cit.*, p. 58. Cf. *Journals*, 503.

16 *Journals*, 244.

17 *Ibid.*, 245.

18 *Ibid.*, 90 (translation modified).

19 *Op. cit.*, p. 69.

20 *Journals*, 101.

21 *Ibid.*, 103.

22 *Ibid.*, 108.

23 *Ibid.*, 109.

24 *Ibid.*, 53.

25 *Ibid.*, 140.

26 *Ibld.*, 61.

27 Cf. J. Hohlenberg, *op. cit.*, p. 73.

28 *Journals*, 149.

29 *Ibid.*, 153.

30 Cf. W. Lowrie, *op. cit.*, p. 106.

31 *Journals*, 119.

32 Quoted *Journals*, p. 44n. from Raphael Meyer's *Kierkegaardske Papirer*, *Forlovelsen*, 1904.

33 *Journals*, 127.

34 Quoted in W. Lowrie, *op. cit.*, p. 197.

35 According to Johannes Hohlenberg, *op. cit.*, p. 81, the five hundred *rigsdaler* a year given to him by his father corresponded to the salary of a young university professor.

36 *Journals*, 1333.

37 *Ibid.*, 207.

38 *Ibid.*, 215.

39 Quoted by T. H. Croxall in *Johannes Climacus*, p. 37, and translated from *Breve og Aktstykker*, which also contain the examiners' official reports on Kierkegaard's performance.

Chapter 2

1 *Journals*, 49 (1836).

2 Cf. Hohlenberg, *op. cit.*, pp. 68, 72.

3 *Journals*, 106.

4 Cf. *Papirer*, II, B, 1–21. Some critics see in this piece a parody of Goethe's *Faust*. Cf. Karl Roos, *Kierkegaard og Goethe*, Copenhagen, 1955, pp. 131–74.

5 Hohlenberg, *op. cit.*, p. 66.

6 *Journals*, 177.

7 *S.V.*, I, 34

8 *Søren Kierkegaard's Pilgrimage to Jutland* (translated by T. H. Croxall), p. 33. There are some extracts in *Journals*, 324–42.

9 *Pilgrimage*, p. 32. Cf. *Journals*, 331.

10 *Journals*, 338.

11 *Pilgrimage*, pp. 35–6.

12 *Ibid.*, p. 36.
13 *Journals*, 335.
14 Quoted from W. Lowrie, *op. cit.*, p. 207.
15 Cf. J. Hohlenberg, *op. cit.*, p. 92.
16 *Ibid.*, p. 101.
17 *Journals*, 160.
18 *Johannes Climacus*, p. 40.
19 Cf. Lowrie, *op. cit.*, p. 143. Cf. *supra*, p. 13.
20 See *The Concept of Irony with constant reference to Socrates* (translated by Lee M. Capell), especially pp. 351–7, for a survey of the various interpretations.
21 *Journals*, 115.
22 *Ibid.*, 164.
23 *Ibid.*, 913.
24 *Ibid.*, 90.
25 *Ibid.*, 574.
26 *Ibid.*, 180.
27 *Ibid.*, 315.
28 *Papirer*, X (3)A 477.
29 *Op. cit.*, p. 222.

Chapter 3

1 Lowrie, *op. cit.*, p. 207.
2 *Ibid.*, p. 218.
3 *Ibid.*, p. 222–3.
4 *Journals*, 392 (translation modified).
5 *Ibid.*, p. 104.
6 Cf. his comment in *The Point of View*, p. 18, where he says that 'religiously he was already in the cloister'.
7 *Journals*, 1278.
8 *Ibid.*, 641.
9 In this and the following chapter the volume and page number after a quotation refer to the English translation of the work discussed, full details of which are given in the bibliography.
10 Cf. *supra*, p. 18.
11 *Journals*, 469.
12 Cf. *Journals*, 448, where Antigone is linked up with 'Nebuchadnezzar's Dream' as well as with 'Solomon and David', two episodes directly inspired by Kierkegaard's relations with his father. See *infra.*, p. 50f.
13 *Papirer*, III B, 45 (2), and III B, 162 (2), for an idea that is barely hinted at in the final text (I, 348).

Chapter 4

1 Cf. *Journals*, 426, for an important criticism of Descartes.
2 *Concluding Unscientific Postscript*, p. 281.
3 Cf. *Fear and Trembling*, p. ix.
4 *Journals*, 439.
5 *Ibid.*, 444.
6 *Ibid.*, 440.
7 *Ibid.*, 444.
8 As T. H. Croxall (*Kierkegaard Commentary*, p. 127, n.2) points

out the original pseudonym was called 'Victorinus Constantinus de bona speranza', which was clearly intended to
indicate Kierkegaard's eventual hope of winning back Regine.
The 'Constantinus' suggests the unswerving quality of his love.

9   *Journals*, 474.
10   *Repetition*, p. xxx.
11   *Journals*, 965.
12   *Point of View*, p. 21.

Chapter 5

1   *Op. cit.*, pp. 188, 208, 228, 326.
2   *Ibid.*, pp. 295, 323.
3   Cf. *Journals*, 431. 'After my death no one will find among my
     papers a single explanation as to what really filled my life (that
     is my consolation); no one will find the words which explain
     everything and which often made what the world would call a
     bagatelle into an event of tremendous importance to me, and
     what I look upon as something insignificant when I take away
     the secret gloss which explains all.'
4   A useful summary of several of these psychological explanations
     is to be found in Marguerite Grimault, *La Mélancolie de
     Kierkegaard*, Paris, 1965. Particularly important is H. Helweg,
     S. Kierkegaard: En psykiatrisk-psykologisk studie, Copenhagen,
     1933.
5   *Journals*, 600.
6   *Ibid.*, 462.
7   *Ibid.*, 670.
8   *Ibid.*, 1288.
9   Quoted in *Journals*, pp. 548–9.
10   Cf. Carl Saggau, *Skyldig-ikke skyldig? Et par kapitler af
     Michael og Søren Kierkegaards Ungdomsliv*, Copenhagen,
     1958.
11   Cf. P. A. Heiberg, *En Episode i Søren Kierkegaards Ungdomsliv*,
     Copenhagen, 1912.
12   *Journals*, 243.
13   *Ibid.*, 447.
14   C. Saggau, *op. cit.*, p. 61.
15   *Journals*, 681.
16   *Ibid.*, 557. Cf. also 525–7.
17   Cf. W. Lowrie, *op. cit.*, p. 22.
18   *Point of View*, p. 78.
19   *Journals*, 359.
20   T. H. Croxall, *Commentary*, pp. xiv, n.2.
21   *Journals*, 937.
22   *Ibid.*, 600.
23   *Ibid.*, 244.
24   *Ibid.*, 600, 806.
25   Cf. on this point Hermann Diem, *Kierkegaard's Dialectic of
     Existence*, and *Journals* (Hong), 1, 350–4 ('Dialectic',
     'Dialectical').
26   *Journals*, 806.
27   *Ibid.*, 447.

Chapter 6

1 We follow current usage in translating *Angst* (*Angest* in Kierke-gaard's time) as 'dread', even though it is only a rough equivalent.
2 *Journals*, 484, where he adds: 'I always stand in an altogether poetic relationship to my works and I am, therefore, a pseudonym'.
3 Cf. Lowrie, *op. cit.*, pp. 143–4.
4 *Journals*, 444.
5 *Ibid.*, 754.
6 *Stages on Life's Way*, pp. 342–3.
7 *Op. cit.*, I, 128–9.
8 *Journals*, 404. Cf. also *Concept of Dread*, p. 145n.
9 *Ibid.*, 402.
10 *Ibid.*, 825.
11 *Ibid.*, 673.

Chapter 7

1 Cf. C. Jørgensen, *S. Kierkegaard, En Biografi* (5 vols., Copen-hagen, 1964), II, 57, who suggests that some notes in the *Papirer* (VI, A 46–52) may belong to this stay in Berlin.
2 *Breve og Akstykker*, I, 143.
3 *Philosophical Fragments*, p. 50.
4 *Journals*, 396, 488.
5 *Ibid.*, 590.
6 *Postscript*, p. 33.
7 Cf. *Either/Or*, II, 277ff.
8 *Postscript*, p. 267.
9 For Kierkegaard's relationship with Hegel, see N. Thulstrup, *Kierkegaards forhold til Hegel og til den spekulative Idealisme indtil 1846*, Copenhagen, 1967, and a useful section in J. Wahl, *Etudes Kierkegaardiennes*, pp. 86–171.
10 *Journals*, 206.
11 *Ibid.*, 633.
12 *Point of View*, p. 131.
13 *Ibid.*, pp. 119–20.
14 Quoted in Hohlenberg, pp. 189–90.
15 *Last Years*, p. 100.

Chapter 8

1 *Op. cit.*, pp. 225–66. At the very end of the *Postscript* (pp. 551–4), Kierkegaard made 'a first and last declaration' in which he publicly acknowledged that he was the author of the works he had previously attributed to pseudonyms.
2 An authoritative study of Kierkegaard's financial position is to be found in Frithiof Brandt and Else Rammel, *Søren Kierke-gaard og Pengene*, Copenhagen, 1935.
3 Cf. J. Hohlenberg, *op. cit.*, pp. 158f.
4 *Journals*, 627.
5 *Ibid.*, 867.
6 *S.V.*, XIV, 7–102. A part has been translated and published as *The Present Age* (along with *Two Minor Ethico-Religious*

Treatises), translated A. Dru and W. Lowrie, Oxford, 1940. The first section contains a review of a novel *Two Ages*, which, although published anonymously, was by Fru Thomasine Gyllembourg, the mother of the well-known writer, J. L. Heiberg.

7   *The Present Age*, p. 92.
8   *Journals*, 747-8.
9   *Ibid.*, 749.
10 *Ibid.*
11 See the introduction to *Crisis in the Life of an Actress, and other essays on Drama*, translated by Stephen Crites, New York, 1967.
12 See 'Kierkegaard and Scribe', in Ronald Grimsley, *Søren Kierkegaard and French Literature*, 1966, pp. 112-29.
13 *Papirer*, X (1) A 402.
14 *Breve og Akstykker*, I, 228.
15 *Ibid.*, I, 225-7 and comments in II, 94-5.
16 *Journals*, 958.
17 *Papirer*, X (2) A 25.
18 C. Jørgensen, *op. cit.*, III, 59.
19 Cf. *supra*, p. 26.
20 *Ibid.*, 878 and *Papirer*, X (6) B 83-102, for a fuller account. See also J. Hohlenberg, *op. cit.*, pp. 210f. for further details of Kierkegaard's relationship with Nielsen.
21 *Journals*, 878.
22 Quoted in Lowrie, *op. cit.*, p. 462.
23 Cf. Lowrie, *loc. cit.*
24 Quoted in Hohlenberg, *op. cit.*, p. 226.
25 Regine outlived Kierkegaard by nearly fifty years. She died in 1904 at the age of eighty-two.

Chapter 9
1   *Journals*, 936.

Chapter 10
1   *Journals*, 807.
2   *Ibid.*, 1023.
3   *Ibid.*, 501.
4   Cf. 'Kierkegaard and Pascal' in Ronald Grimsley, *Søren Kierkegaard and French Literature*, pp. 73-88.
5   *Journals*, 627.
6   *Ibid.*, 969.
7   *Ibid.*, 1001.
8   *Ibid.*, 1298.
9   *Ibid.*, 1252.
10 *Ibid.*, 1294.
11 *Ibid.*, 1288.
12 *Ibid.*, 1296, and cf. Lowrie, *op. cit.*, p. 567.
13 For this article and all the others on the same subject, see *Kierkegaard's Attack upon 'Christendom'*, 1854-55 (translated W. Lowrie).
14 *Ibid.*, p. 8.
15 *Ibid.*, p. 55.

16 The discourse is included in *For Self-Examination – Judge for Yourselves*, pp. 223–60.
17 *Journals*, 1310.
18 *Ibid.*, 1319.
19 Frithiof Brandt, *Søren Kierkegaard (1813–55), his life, his works*, p. 101.
20 Cf. T. H. Croxall, *Glimpses and Impressions of Kierkegaard*, pp. 74–5.
21 *Ibid.*, p. 111.
22 *Journals*, p. 550.
23 *Ibid.*, 1275, 1371.

Bibliography

The most comprehensive bibliography of Kierkegaard studies is:
Himmelstrup, J., *Søren Kierkegaard, International Bibliografi*,
Copenhagen, 1962.

A: Kierkegaard's Works

1: DANISH SOURCES

The main Danish sources for the study of Kierkegaard's work are:
Søren Kierkegaards Samlede Vaerker, 3rd ed., edited by A. B.
Drachman, J. L. Heiberg & H. O. Lange, P. H. Rohde, 20 vols.,
Copenhagen.
Søren Kierkegaards Papirer, ed. by P. A. Heiberg, V. Kuhr, E.
Torsting, and N. Thulstrup, 22 vols., Copenhagen, 1968–70.
Breve og Aktstykker vedrørende Søren Kierkegaard, edited by N.
Thulstrup, 2 vols., Copenhagen, 1953–4.

2: ENGLISH TRANSLATIONS OF KIERKEGAARD'S WORKS

The date in brackets after each title is that of the original Danish
edition.
The Concept of Irony with constant reference to Socrates, (Disserta-
tion for the Master's degree, 1841), translated with an introduction
and notes by Lee M. Capell, New York, 1965.
Either/Or, A Fragment of Life. By Victor Eremita (1843): translated
by D. F. Swenson, L. M. Swenson, W. Lowrie, 2 vols., Princeton,
1944.
    New edition with revisions by H. A. Johnson, 2 vols., Anchor
Books, New York, 1959.
Johannes Climacus, or De Omnibus Dubitandum Est (written 1842/3
and left unfinished): *and a Sermon* (1844), translated with an
assessment by T. H. Croxall, London, 1958.
Edifying Discourses (1843/4), translated by D. F. Swenson, L. M.
Swenson, 4 vols., Minneapolis, 1943–5 (2 volume edition in
1962).
Repetition, An Essay in Experimental Psychology, by Constantine
Constantius (1843), translated by W. Lowrie, Princeton, 1941.
Fear and Trembling. A Dialectical Lyric, by Johannes de Silentio
(1843), translated by R. Payne, London, 1939.
Philosophical Fragments or a Fragment of Philosophy, by Johannes
Climacus. Responsible for publication: S. Kierkegaard (1844),
translated D. F. Swenson, Princeton, 1936.
    Translation revised by H. Hong, with a new introduction and
commentary by N. Thulstrup, Princeton, 1962.
*The Concept of Dread. A Simple psychological deliberation oriented in
the direction of the dogmatic problem of original sin*, by Vigilius

Haufniensis (1844), translated by W. Lowrie, Princeton, 1944. (Translation revised by H. A. Johnson, 1957.)

Thoughts on Crucial Situations in Human Life: Three Discourses on Imagined Occasions (1845), translated D. F. & L. M. Swenson, Minneapolis, 1941.

Stages on Life's Way. Studies by Sundry persons. Collected, forwarded to the press and published by Hilarius Bookbinder, translated by W. Lowrie, Princeton, 1940.

Concluding Unscientific Postscript to the Philosophical Fragments. A mimetic-pathetic-dialectical composition, an existential contribution, by Johannes Climacus, published by S. Kierkegaard (1846). Translated by D. F. Swenson and W. Lowrie, London, 1941.

On Authority and Revelation. The Book on Adler, or a Cycle of Ethico-Religious Essays (written 1846/7: not published), translated W. Lowrie, Princeton, 1955.

Edifying Discourses in a different vein (1841), translated by A. S. Aldworth and W. S. Ferrie.

    1. *Purify your hearts* (London, 1937).
    2. *Consider the Lilies* (London, 1940).
    3. *The Gospel of Sufferings* (London, 1955).

The Works of Love (1847), translated D. F. Swenson, L. M. Swenson, London, 1946.

    [Another edition with a translation by H. E. Hong, New York, 1962].

Christian Discourses (1848), *The Lilies of the Field and the Birds of the Air* (1849), and *Three Discourses at the Communion on Fridays* ('The High Priest' – 'The Publican' – 'The Woman who was a Sinner') (1849), translated by W. Lowrie, London–New York, 1939.

The Present Age, and *Two Minor Ethico-Religious Treatises*, by H. H. (1848). Translated by A. Dru, W. Lowrie, London–New York, 1940.

The Crisis and a Crisis in the Life of an Actress, by Inter et Inter: and other essays on drama, translated by Stephen D. Crites, New York, 1967.

The Sickness unto Death. A Christian Psychological Exposition for Edification and Awakening by Anti-Climacus, edited by S. Kierkegaard (1849). Translated by W. Lowrie, London, 1941.

The Point of View for my Work as an Author. Two Notes about 'The Individual', and *On My Work as an Author* (1848–51). Translated by W. Lowrie, London, 1939.

Armed Neutrality, and *An Open Letter*. With relevant selections from the *Journals* and *Papers*, edited and translated with an introduction by H. V. and E. H. Hong. Background essay and commentary by G. Malantschuk, Indiana, 1968.

For Self-Examination : Judge for Yourselves! together with *Two Discourses at the Communion on Fridays* (1851); *The Unchangeableness of God; An Address* (1855). Translated W. Lowrie, Oxford, 1941.

Kierkegaard's Attack on 'Christendom' (1854–5) (articles in *The Fatherland* and *The Instant*, together with two short pamphlets). Translated W. Lowrie, Oxford, 1944.

Training in Christianity by Anti-Climacus, edited by S. Kierke-
gaard (1850), and the *Discourse* 'accompanying it'. Translated
W. Lowrie, 1946.
The Prayers of Kierkegaard, edited with a new introduction to his
life and thought by P. D. Lefevre. Chicago, 1956.
Meditations from Kierkegaard, edited and translated by T. H.
Croxall, Philadelphia, 1955.

SELECTIONS FROM THE JOURNALS AND PAPERS:

The Journals of Søren Kierkegaard, translated and edited by A. Dru,
Oxford–New York, 1938.
S. Kierkegaard: The Last Years, Journals 1853–1855, edited and
translated by R. Gregor Smith, London, 1965.
Søren Kierkegaard's Journals and Papers. Vol. I, A–E: Vol II, F–K;
edited and translated by H. V. and E. H. Hong, assisted by G.
Malantschuk, Bloomington–London, 1967, 1970.
The Diary of S. Kierkegaard, edited by P. H. Rohde, translated by
G. M. Anderson, New York, 1950.
Søren Kierkegaard's Pilgrimage to Jutland, prepared by Arthur
Dahl and translated by T. H. Croxall, Danish Tourist Association,
Copenhagen, 1948.

SELECTIONS FROM KIERKEGAARD'S WORKS:

A Kierkegaard Anthology, edited by R. Bretell, Princeton, 1946.
Kierkegaard, selected and introduced by W. H. Auden, London,
1955.

B: Critical Works in English
ALLEN, E. L., *Kierkegaard, his Life and Thought*, London, 1935.
ARBAUGH, G. E., and G. B., *Kierkegaard's Authorship. A Guide to the
Writings of Kierkegaard*, London, 1968.
BAIN, J. A., *S. Kierkegaard, his Life and Teaching*, London, 1935.
BRANDT, FRITHIOF, *Søren Kierkegaard, 1813–1855; his Life; his
Works*, translated by A. R. Born, Copenhagen, 1963.
CHANNING-PEARCE, M., *The Terrible Crystal*, London, 1940.
CHESTOV, L., *Kierkegaard and the Existential Philosophy* (translated
E. Hewitt), Ohio, 1969.
COLE, J. PRESTON, *The Problematic Self in Kierkegaard and Freud*,
New Haven, 1971.
COLLINS, JAMES, *The Mind of Kierkegaard*, Chicago, 1953.
CROXALL, T. H., *Kierkegaard Studies*, London and Redhill, 1948.
        Kierkegaard Commentary, London, 1956.
            Glimpses and Impressions of Kierkegaard, London,
            1959.
DIEM, H., *Kierkegaard's Dialectic of Existence* (translated H.
Knight), Edinburgh, 1959.
DRU, A., *Søren Kierkegaard*, London, 1936.
DUPRÉ, LOUIS, *Kierkegaard as Theologian*, London, 1964.
ELLER, VERNARD, *Kierkegaard and Radical Discipleship: A New
Perspective*, Princeton, 1968.

FRIEDMANN, R., *Kierkegaard; the analysis of the psychological personality*, London, 1949.

FULFORD, F. W., *S. A. Kierkegaard, a Study*, London, 1908.

GARELICK, H. M., *The Anti-Christianity of Kierkegaard, a Study of 'Concluding Unscientific Postscript'*, The Hague, 1965.

GATES, JOHN A., *Christendom Revisited: A Kierkegaardian View of the Church Today*, London, 1967.
The Life and Thought of Kierkegaard for Everyman, Philadelphia, 1960.

GEISMAR, E., *Lectures on the religious thought of Søren Kierkegaard*, Minneapolis, 1937.

GEORGE, A. G., *The First Sphere. A Study in Kierkegaardian Aesthetics*, London, 1965.

GRIMSLEY, RONALD, *Søren Kierkegaard and French Literature*, Cardiff, 1966.

HAECKER, T., *Kierkegaard the Cripple*, translated C. Van O. Bruyn, Oxford, 1948.
Søren Kierkegaard, translated A. Dru, Oxford, 1937.

HOHLENBERG, JOHANNES, *Søren Kierkegaard*, translated T. H. Croxall, London, 1954.

(ed.) H. JOHNSON and N. THULSTRUP, *A Kierkegaard Critique*, New York, 1962.

JOLIVET, R., *Introduction to Kierkegaard* (translated W. H. Barber), New York, 1951.

LOWRIE, WALTER, *Kierkegaard*, London, 1938.
A Short Life of Kierkegaard, Oxford, 1943.

MALANTSCHUK, G., *Kierkegaard's Way to the Truth*, translated M. Michelsen, Minneapolis, 1963.

MARTIN, H. V., *Kierkegaard the Melancholy Dane*, New York, 1950.

MILLER, L. L., *In Search of the Self: the Individual in the thought of Kierkegaard*, Philadelphia, 1962.

PATRICK, D. G. M., *Pascal and Kierkegaard*, 2 vols, London and Redhill, 1947.

PRICE, GEORGE, *The Narrow Pass*, London, 1963.

ROHDE, P. P. *Søren Kierkegaard*, New York, 1963.

ROOS, H., *Kierkegaard and Catholicism*, translated R. M. Braeckett, Westminster, 1934.

SPONHEIM, Paul, *Kierkegaard on Christ and Christian Coherence*, London, 1968.

SWENSON, D. F., *Something about Kierkegaard* (ed. L. M. Swenson), 2nd ed., Minneapolis, 1945.

THOMAS, J. HEYWOOD, *Subjectivity and Paradox*, Oxford, 1957.

THOMSON, JOSIAH, *The Lonely Labyrinth: Kierkegaard's Pseudonymous Works*, Carbondale: Edwardsville, Southern Illinois University Press, 1967.

THOMTE, REIDAR, *Kierkegaard's Philosophy of Religion*, Princeton, 1948.

WYSCHOGROD, M., *Kierkegaard and Heidegger*, New York, 1954.

ZUIDEMA, S. U., *Kierkegaard*, translated D. H. Freeman, Grand Rapids, 1960.

Index